With Wings:

An Anthology of Literature by Women with Disabilities

EDITED BY
MARSHA SAXTON and
FLORENCE HOWE

Published by VIRAGO PRESS Limited 1988
20-23 Mandela Street, Camden Town, London NW1 OHQ

First published by The Feminist Press at The City University of New York 1987

British Library Cataloguing in Publication Data

With wings : an anthology of literature by
women with disabilities.
1. Physically handicapped women – Personal
observations – Collections
I. Saxton, Marsha   II. Howe, Florence
362.4'092'2

ISBN 0–86068–166–1

Printed by Cox & Wyman Ltd, Reading, Berkshire.

Contents

Preface to the British edition
Preface
Introduction

Preface to the British edition

I was excited about being asked to write a British preface for this book – not least because unbeknown to those who had recommended me for the job, Marsha Saxton and I know each other through our work in the disability field and co-counselling. As Marsha said, in response to my letter telling her I'd been offered and had accepted the task, the fact that able-bodied women should have linked us is encouraging because it really makes it clear that there is a viable international disability movement.

As with every oppressed group, our oppression and therefore our reactions to it are similar in all societies that are run on the same economic lines. This really helps the development of an international movement, because even across quite markedly different cultures we can speak to each other in a common language of experience. I shall, then, look first at the overall similarities in American and British society before I move on to my personal reactions to voices I recognise in this powerful book, and then to the cultural differences that add a spice of variety to our trans-Atlantic lives.

Before I do, though, a word about terminology. For the purpose of this piece I have decided to adopt the phrase 'physically challenged' instead of disabled, or any of the more commonly used terms. This is partly because, having thought I liked it for theoretical reasons, I wanted to find out what it felt like to use it extensively, and partly because I wanted to prompt other people's reactions to it. Briefly, I like it because it refers both to the bodily reality, and to the barriers thrown up by society in our paths.

It doesn't take a skilled political analyst to see that the economic and political characters of the (not-very-) United States and the (hardly-at-all-) United Kingdom are increasingly alike. People who are physically challenged are pushed aside in a system that is based on the fastest possible production of wealth by the masses for the few. Add to this the nauseous brew of sexism and ever-decreasing job opportunities and you have a magic formula for performing a vanishing trick on us female crips ... or you would have if we hadn't already found our voices. It is worth pondering a little on how we have found our individual and collective voices. All governments have the resources to support the physically challenged if they choose to, but the British and US governments are wealthy enough (given the past and present plunder of resources from other countries and the exploitation of workers throughout) to have given many of us considerable financial and/or technological assistance. This, especially in the form of money or cars for transport and equipment for communication, means that it has become practically possible to meet. When we meet we inevitably share our experience, and learn and grow at both a political and personal level.

Another factor in common is the women's movement. Many of us physically challenged women found our political selves through what we learnt from the women's movement. We applied the model of oppression to our own situation and discovered a powerful tool for understanding our experience. We grasped the strength to be gained from sharing how we came to be who we are, in a supportive as opposed to a competitive atmosphere, and went after it.

These voices of ours, these wings, are perhaps at their strongest in the arts at present. In England – and I believe in Scotland, Wales and Ireland too – it is through the entire spectrum of the arts that the disability movement is most vibrantly exploring and expressing itself, ourselves and our culture. We physically challenged women are pop singers, painters, actresses, musicians, dancers, poets, sculptors ... you name it, we're doing it. (My good friend Nancy Willis, whose work graces the front cover of this book, is one of our foremost artists.) Just like the women in this book, some choose to represent disability in their art, others do not. Many do both. We may neither expect nor receive good reviews from the male able-bodied establishment, but who cares when the audience is cheering?

The arts aside though (and what proportion of us can earn enough from it?), the economic system sketched earlier necessarily consigns most of us to the scrap-heap of living on state or private charity. Increasingly we have reverted to having to look to private, particularly family sources of charity, as our governments withdraw further and further from even acknowledging their responsibilities. Here in Britain, for instance, we have just undergone changes in the benefits system which have left many people who are physically challenged in financial crisis. At the same time, the attempt to improve our employment opportunities that was contained in the Contract Compliance legislation* has been scrapped, so that even more of us are likely to have to depend on the few pennies the state now cares to throw our way. The fundamental social and psychological effects are identical on both sides of the Atlantic, and different details are of interest but of no great importance. There is, however, one major and significant difference between our two societies, and I believe it has led to American superiority in provision and

* Contract Compliance required contracted firms to improve their employment of physically challenged people (and others) or have their contracts cancelled.

progress in many states: the Americans have a constitution which provides an official and accepted framework of reference for social development. This means that people who are physically challenged have solid ground from which to fight for their rights (as do all oppressed groups there) and no matter how hard or how long the fight, it is firmly bolstered by that precious constitution. Here in Britain we have almost no recourse to and no guiding hand for the law. It has not, does not and will not silence us, but it does make it more of an uphill struggle, and we frequently have to start all over again, just to establish our most basic rights.

So. Here we are with not dissimilar circumstances and therefore familiar stories, ones with which those of us with similar disabilities can particularly identify. Personally I responded with soul-deep harmonies to several contributions in this book. One was Roberta Chepko's story of how her mother used to make the unbearable (shopping for shoes) bearable by turning the trips into family visits to MacDonald's. My Mum would do the same thing; after hospital appointments, which were tedious at the best and thoroughly alarming at the worst, she'd take me (and my sister when it was in school holidays) to what was then Lyons Corner House for a delicious cake and a drink. I'm shedding grateful tears as I write about it and I bet neither of our mothers realised how perfectly these seemingly small gestures made us feel that someone understood how hard and lonely it can sometimes be. I love my mother dearly for it.

Other contributions that spoke most to me were those about chronic illness. I've had one now for a couple of years and I've realised how alike reactions are to this and to what we more commonly term disability. For instance, if ever we can't cope, we are blamed for that. We must have done the wrong thing, or eaten the wrong thing, or not done the right thing. If we do make our needs clear *and* if we don't (but look like we may need something) we are being too demanding. The demands on us, apparently, are of no account, especially (I tremble to question it, unworthy crip that I am) the demand that as women we should be fit enough to be nurturing everyone else. My own experience, together with various contributions in this book, emphatically confirms my previous assumption that chronic illness and disability can most usefully be considered together. It is not a sloppiness, nor a mere reluctance to exclude anyone, that has prompted the editors to do this.

I am impressed, in fact, by the tremendous respect shown by Marsha Saxton and Florence Howe in their selection and presentation of pieces. No disability gets a higher rank or billing than any other, nor do we get a sense that one person is more valued than any other. This may seem a small thing to anyone outside the disability arena, but our oppression has divided us from each other in numerous ways, so that the very act of bringing us together across disabilities, and across literary standing, is a unifying and healing one.

Moving on to evident differences between the States and Britain, there's one thing that struck me forcibly as I read this book, and that is that unlike much British writing by women who are physically challenged, humour is a little used tool within these pages. In my many conversations with women here who do use a lot of humour both verbally and in their writing, I have found a common explanation. We have to develop it to combat the air of tragedy that people adopt around us. I am left wondering whether perhaps the same thing does not happen across the water. Could it be that, quite the reverse, the American response to disability is to demonstrate a hale and hearty, pioneering lack of concern? This would certainly push physically challenged people to communicate very seriously about their situation. Or is it perhaps a wider cultural difference? Invitations to the States to see at first hand are more than welcome, especially if a ticket comes with the invite!

I have the impression, though again I may be wrong, that there is a feature of the British culture which saves us from the worst devastations of reactions to being visibly disabled: the Great British Tradition of Eccentricity. It doesn't make us immune to the assault of the cult of the body-beautiful, but it does give us perhaps a little more leeway than our American cousins to be proud of looking different. For that relief much thanks, since it is all too easy to look across the water and decide that we are light years behind . . . I mean, Marsha writes to me from the State Office of Handicapped Affairs. Well, jokes about all affairs being handicapped aside, such an organisation is unheard of here, especially when people who are physically challenged are at the helm. Without a doubt, the return of the Vietnam war wounded pushed our cause ahead in the States with unprecedented force, because the collective American conscience could not tolerate shoving that many people aside. Unhappily the British war in the Malvinas was successfully portrayed as a triumph and anyway was short and did not result in so many casualties, otherwise some good might have come out of an otherwise sickening event. To those of our men who did come back disabled I say – there are some of us at least who have not forgotten you. Even the war we are pretending not to wage in Northern Ireland, which has dragged on and on, and which does somewhat resemble the Vietnam story, has not had the same effect. Of course our men are not sent in the same numbers, but still, unless we are not being told the truth (impossible, impossible) they all either survive intact or are killed outright . . . (As I correct the proofs of this piece, startling evidence of the surpression of facts about, and lack of support for, our Malvinas war-wounded is emerging in revelations about veteran Robert Lawrence. A wounded ex-officer in the Scots Guards, Lawrence claims a Government campaign has now been launched to discredit him.

Another rather different point is that one should be aware that when a writer speaks of her limitations, she may be offering us what she *feels* is an insuperable barrier rather than one that is in fact so. One example would be Frances Deloatch's repetition of the doctor's assertion that she is too small to have a baby. I have two women friends who have the same syndrome (brittle bone disease) and who are no bigger than Frances. One now has a four-year-old who also has the syndrome,

Preface to the British edition

while the other has two able-bodied children. Oh for the ability to know when our doctors are talking through their arses, and then to know who to turn to who will actually think.

I'd like to finish by throwing out some challenges. I mentioned earlier the importance of the women's movement in nurturing the much younger disability movement. Is it perhaps the lack of a similar model for men that has meant we have not yet seen an anthology by men who are physically challenged? You men have a different experience. It is no less valid and no less important, so let's be reading our men's perspective — and soon!

Also I want to put together contributions from particular groups of women in this country who have as yet not had a platform for exploring their experiences. I'm particularly interested in hearing from women who are physically challenged and whose children are too; from Afro-Caribbean and Asian women who want to look at the special meaning of being physically challenged in their communities, and from physically challenged women who sense that they have experience in any other area that has yet to have a public airing.

As you read this book, you will see that there are thousands of facets to our existence; never was there a more misleadingly simple expression than 'the disabled', nor could it be much more firmly laid to rest than with this anthology.

Merry Cross
London, 1988

Below is a list of those organisations run by and for physically challenged women in England. This list was not readily available and is most probably incomplete. In the time available I have been unable to ascertain definitely whether there are such groups in Ireland, Scotland & Wales, however the contacts I have suggest not – as yet. I intend compiling a complete list for the future and then circulating it to appropriate organisations to ensure that it is easy to come by. So if you belong to a group not listed here, please let me know c/o Virago Press.

But *please* read any accompanying notes, because some groups only want to be contacted by physically challenged women themselves.

Manchester Disabled Women's Group,
c/o 14 Clovelly Road,
Chorlton,
MANCHESTER 21 2XW.

Women With Disabilities Group,
c/o Ann Saunders
Equal Opps. & Race Relations Dept.,
Community Liaison & Development,
Derbyshire Co. Council,
    County Offices,
Matlock,
DERBYSHIRE D4 3AG.
This group is just forming.

Preface to the British edition

Winvisible (Women with visible and invisible disabilities)
King's Cross Women's Centre,
71 Tonbridge Street,
LONDON WC1 49DZ.

Gemma (an organisation for lesbian women with and without disabilities)
BM Box 5700,
LONDON WC1N 3XX.

Feminist Audio Books (a feminist tape library)
52-54 Featherstone Street,
LONDON, EC1.

Women's Tape Over (pressure group putting out a taped monthly digest from the feminist press)
c/o Alison Behr,
72 Alpine Road,
LONDON SE16 2RD.

The London Deaf Women's Group
c/o Geraldine O'Halloran,
The Huddleston Centre,
30 Powell Road,
Hackney,
LONDON E5.
This group is newly formed, but is expecting to expand rapidly outside London.

Disabled Mother's Group
Disability Resource Centre,
1A Warner Road,
Walthamstow,
LONDON E17.

Disabled Women in Greenwich
c/o Anne Rae,
Flat 2,
98 Woodhill,
Woolwich,
LONDON SE18.

Women with Disabilities
Hackney Women's Centre,
20 Dalston Lane,
LONDON E8.
This group will not welcome inquiries or mailings from anyone other than women with disabilities.

Bristol Women With Disabilities Group
c/o IDEA,
William House,
101 Eden Vale Road,
Westbury,
WILTS. BA13 3QF.

U.P.I.A.S Women's Group
c/o 56 Thanet Street,
Clay Cross,
Chesterfield,
DERBYSHIRE S45 9JT.

The following is a contact address for anyone interested in a women's disability group in Eire.
Nuala Cadwell,
96 Trees Road,
Mt. Merrion,
Co. Dublin,
EIRE.

Preface

With Wings is an anthology of stories, poems, and essays by thirty women writers, all of whom have a disability or physical difference. The volume was compiled with several goals in mind:

1. To combat educational discrimination, both sexist and "able-bodiest," against disabled women and girls, by providing a fine literary volume that presents and celebrates the talent, strengths, and creative abilities of this group, until now virtually ignored as a group;
2. To enhance the self-esteem of disabled women and girls by presenting positive role models of the disabled female as literary artist, communicator, and leader of her own movement;
3. To provide a literary forum for the exploration of the experiences of disabled women, white or members of minority groups, heterosexual or lesbian, and of different social classes;
4. To challenge the literary community to follow suit by recognizing works by disabled women, and;
5. To create a literary volume that encourages readers to confront their *own* feelings about physical limitations, appearance, and standards of beauty, about dependence and vulnerability.

The book is divided into three thematic parts. In Part 1, Living in These Bodies, These Minds, works describe the physical and emotional experience of disability. In Part 2, Seeking Help and Love, selections place disability in the context of relationships, and explore such themes as love, sexuality, and interdependence. Part 3, Transcendence, contains works about surmounting barriers, both societal and internal, and about reevaluating and challenging traditional concepts about being female and disabled.

With Wings is the result of a three-year collaboration between the Boston Self-Help Center and The Feminist Press at The City University of New York. A grant from the Women's Educational Equity Act Program of the U.S. Department of Education offered support to conduct an extensive literature search and call for manuscripts in the far-reaching and often remote community of disabled women, and then contributed to the making of this book.

At the onset of the project, the editors hoped for the broadest representation of types of disabilities and of women's life experiences relating to disability. We quickly came to realize the difficulties in achieving this goal. In a single volume, we could not possibly include every disability (depending on how one classifies, there are many thousands of disabling conditions), nor cover all the important issues disabled women face. After careful consideration, the scope was defined to include those conditions that directly affect such fundamental activities as walking, seeing, hearing, breathing, self-care, dexterity, learning; and to include such physical differences in appearance as scarring, which, in our society, also may be disabling for women. We also chose to include chronic pain and illness within the definition of disability. Many women with conditions such as arthritis, cancer, heart disease, or multiple sclerosis become more visibly disabled through the course of the disease, as amputation or weakness requires adaptive devices. Those people who suffer such "hidden" conditions as epilepsy, respiratory illness, or diabetes, also face serious discrimination in all areas of life—employment, housing, personal relationships.

We received many excellent contributions about mental illness, but felt that to include one or two of these works would provide only a superficial exploration of this complex topic. Although learning disabilities are represented in the volume, it was again not possible to explore adequately the wide range of developmental disabilities that affect the lives of countless women. Perhaps this book will serve as a stimulus to the creation of other anthologies.

In the selection process we chose those works of highest literary quality that portrayed the lives of disabled women accurately, addressed important issues, challenged stereotypes, and presented fresh perspectives. We tried to guarantee the broadest possible base of experience by reaching in our search women of different class and ethnic backgrounds, race, age, and sexual preference. We selected works with a feminist perspective and ones from a more traditional viewpoint.

The process of the literature search was an arduous one—disability and illness are often invisible issues in the lives of women. The biographies of women writers often omit completely the fact of their disability; writers themselves have often chosen not to make reference to it, even when their work was an outgrowth of the experience of pain or limitation. The risk of revealing such a stigmatized characteristic may have been too great, the internalization of that stigma too strong. The most effective process turned out to be word of mouth: asking librarians; asking women's studies, ethnic studies, and literary scholars; asking friends who are avid readers, disability rights activists, and helping professionals; asking everyone, "Do you know of any disabled women writers, or writers who write about disability?"

Such a question usually prompted an intense discussion about the nature of such a group, "disabled women." Many had not previously considered the question of the portrayal of disabled women in literature, and, consequently, the literary community touched by this project gained a substantial dose of consciousness-raising, an important side-effect. The call for manuscripts began an exciting process. We mailed 3700 flyers to individuals, organizations, agencies, and networks we knew were interested in the topic, including the mailing lists of the Disability Rights Education Defense Fund, *Kaleidoscope* magazine, and the National Committee on Arts for the Handicapped. In response, we received over 350 submissions of fiction, poetry, and essays (and many hundreds of phone calls from across the United States and Canada).

Reading and reviewing the submissions were formidable tasks as well as exciting ones for the editors, project advisors, and field readers. We offer thanks especially to Barbara Hillyer Davis, Joan Hendrix, Meg Kocher, Maxine McCants, Adrienne Rich, Grace Mattern Shane, and Irving Zola. Special acknowledgment is due also to Bernice Sandler, who first suggested the idea of the anthology. Mark Limont offered loving support and critical suggestions. Joanne O'Hare and Paula J. Martinac of The Feminist Press took time and care in the shaping of the book.

Introduction

Who are women with disabilities? We are a large minority with great diversity. We are women with sensory limitations, mobility impairments, a history of chronic illness, birth defects, and with so-called "hidden" disabilities, including epilepsy and diabetes. We are teenage women and older women and the range between. We are Asian, Native American, black, and white women, and women from all social classes and ethnic groups. It has been estimated that approximately one out of every twelve people in the world is disabled; this means that disability affects the lives of more than two million women.

Consider the following well-known women: Charlotte Bronte, Florence Nightingale, Harriet Tubman, Dorothea Lange, Sarah Bernhardt. How well known is it that each of these women had some variety of disability or chronic illness? Charlotte Bronte, the novelist, and Florence Nightingale, the founder of modern nursing, experienced chronic, periodic weakness requiring bedrest; Harriet Tubman, the abolitionist, was subject to "fainting spells," later believed to be caused by epilepsy; Dorothea Lange, the photographer, had polio, which permanently affected her ability to walk smoothly; and Sarah Bernhardt, the actress, performed with a wooden limb when one of her legs was amputated in her seventies. Because the issue of disability has not often been discussed, even in biographical or historical accounts, contemporary women must search for valuable role models, often fruitlessly. The invisibility hurts us. We miss the pleasure of knowing about women who have lived lives with physical limitations, and achieved success despite being both female and disabled. We need to cease wasting energy hiding our disabilities, and overcompensating for them.

In some ways, all women are affected by stereotypes about physical difference or limitation. We are beset by the media to buy products (some contributing to health problems) that conceal or alter our appearance so we may adhere to rigid cultural standards of beauty. As girls we learn to feel inadequate about our bodies. Almost all of us have experienced some physical illness and injury, and know the frustrations, inconveniences, and the pain this brings. And yet, an important and useful distinction defines the group "women with disabilities." Simply put: these are not temporary frustrations, inconveniences, or pain.

Although the lives of women in our society are often constrained, the lives of disabled women are doubly so. In fact, there are many parallels between the oppression of women and of disabled people. Both groups are seen by others as passive, dependent, and childlike; their skills are minimized and their contributions to society undervalued. Such stereotyping of women who also have physical or sensory disabilities or chronic disease seriously limits their educational and employment opportunities. Disabled women who are members of racial or ethnic minority groups, older women, and lesbians are vulnerable to other stereotypes as well.

Surveys conducted by the U.S. Rehabilitation Services Administration in 1977 show that opportunities for disabled women are more limited than for disabled men. Only 70.9 percent of disabled women are rehabilitated into wage-earning occupations, compared to 97.2 percent of disabled men. Of these, women are directed mainly into service (clerical and "helping") positions, while men are placed in a far wider range of occupational fields.[1] Disabled women also earn substantially lower average weekly wages than men. The 1981 Census revealed that disabled women earn less than 24 cents for each dollar earned by nondisabled men; black disabled women earn 12 cents for each dollar. Disabled women earn approximately 52 percent of what nondisabled women earn. These studies and others in the educational, vocational, and rehabilitation arenas point out the far-reaching effects of discrimination.

In focusing on the experience of disabled *women*, we are asserting the importance of challenging the barriers of sexism as essential to the success of the disability rights movement. The creation of a distinct women's movement within the larger social movement adds power and impetus to the whole. By freeing the power of the women in that group, we challenge the patterns that also limit and distort the humanity, creativity, and strength of disabled men.

Several of the women whose work is included in this book do not consider themselves "disabled," even though they do have a physical difference or limitation. The use of that label must remain a choice for the individual person. The issue is not merely linguistic usage (discussed further in the introduction to Part 1) but rather, identity, self-concept, and the associations such words as "disabled" and "handicapped" carry. For some women the stigma of these labels feels more solidly hurtful than for others.

The women's disability rights movement exists for every woman who needs it, but each woman must decide for herself whether to join. In *No More Stares,* women discuss the implications of defining themselves as "disabled" women as opposed to identifying with other constituencies.[2] One woman, Judy, states:

> Disability is the primary problem in our lives. Once we identify ourselves as powerful disabled individuals, we can go back into our secondary communities, whether it be the black community, the Chicano community, the women's community, or some combination of these. We can go back into our communities and start making them deal with us the way they should be dealing with us.

For another woman, Barbara, it is not so clear:

> I'm a member of three minorities: I'm a woman, Asian, and disabled. Which do I identify with most strongly? It's like a triangle. It depends on the circumstances which point of the triangle is on top.

Based on an individual's life experiences, the triangle may be weighted to fix certain priorities about others. Judy and a third woman, Riua, have different priorities. According to Riua:

> My primary oppression is Black, there is no doubt about that. I am a feminist because I am a woman. I am part of the disabled movement because I am disabled. But I would have to come out of the struggle of Black people to become a total feminist, or to become a person that thinks primarily in terms of disability.

For one woman it may be an important step to "come out" as a disabled person; for another it may depend on the situation. For yet another, "I am no longer disabled." For those who decide to, there is much to gain from taking the identity "female and disabled." Today, there is a growing women's disability rights movement that is defining specific challenges, generating resources, and building strength to combat discrimination. In defining ourselves as "disabled women," we can come together. In meeting with each other, we can find the particular safety to share our feelings with those others "who know what it's like," to express frustrations and refuel energies to challenge limits set before us. Together, we can identify the themes of our common experience, while serving the special needs of individuals among us.

The voices of the women's disability rights movement come from many places. One important series of voices comes from writers, who testify to our progress toward self-expression, self-examination, and self-determinism. Literature is an important and effective tool for education and social change. Literature illuminates the details of daily living, the tiniest aspects of life experience, and at the same time the deepest meanings of this experience. Literature may point out social ills, while offering new possibilities; it communicates pain and transcends it. Literature speaks powerfully and profoundly, as well as subtly, delicately.

The experience of creating offers much to the writer as well as to the reader. The process of writing, the concentrated focus on increasing skill, the need to communicate feelings as well as thoughts, the experience of stretching to achieve the desired result, may itself be empowering. In the process of creating, the writer reexamines and explores herself, releases emotions, and reevaluates her perspectives. This process is supremely useful for disabled women. In our need to name the physical pain, the pain of loss, of limitation, of frustration, and the anger at insensitivity or fear, we want to be heard, acknowledged, heeded. Literary expression offers an extraordinary opportunity. We must sometimes be reminded that the lives of disabled women are worthy of literary attention, that our experiences may make important contributions.

Only recently has the literature written by women begun to receive the attention it deserves. Many new texts and collections have appeared in the past ten years that celebrate women's literary achievements and explore the lives of women writers. Traditional notions, previously male-defined, are being challenged. Women's writing is gaining appreciation for its reflection of the unique themes and conditions of women's lives.

Disabled writers are also beginning to receive attention. Contests and awards supporting the publication of disabled writers' work are being sponsored by major disability services organizations, such as United Cerebral Palsy, and government agencies, including the National Endowment for the Arts. This new attention helps to counteract the historical silencing of our experience.

While it is important to celebrate and publicize such literary work, we must be alert to the stereotype that regards skilled disabled artists as "amazing" and "inspiring." The underlying assumption of such views of disabled people is an expectation that they are not capable at all. Their ability comes as a surprise. That a successful writer may have some physical difference or perceptual limitation is not testimony to superhuman talent; it is an example of the adaptive capabilities of human beings, which allow them to excel in some areas and work around limitations in others. Our society is hungry for inspiration, for heroes and heroines. All of our lives are hard in some ways in this age of stress and uncertainty. We crave a glimpse of transcendence, a chance to overcome the many barriers that *all* of us face. Disabled people with tangible limitations are easy targets for others' search for inspiration. A writer's disability may have interfered with her work. It may have stimulated or contributed to it. Or it may not have affected it at all, at least no more than any of the many other aspects of her life experience. As disabled women writers, we deserve recognition on the merits of our work and because of the skill of our contributions, not *because* we are disabled.

This book is about our lives, the confrontation of particular barriers, and some solutions, some unique viewpoints, some valuable contributions. An anthology is a collection of many voices. *With Wings* provides a rich diversity of talent and perspective. No one contributor can speak for all, but each voice is important and needs to be heard.

NOTES

1. J. Corbette O'Toole and Cece Weeks, *What Happens after School? A Study of Disabled Women in Education.* San Francisco: Women's Educational Equity Communications Network, 1978.

2. *No More Stares.* Berkeley, Calif.: Disability Rights Education Defense Fund, 1981.

With Wings

Part I
Living in These Bodies, These Minds

Virginia Woolf wondered in her 1930 essay "On Being Ill" why there is not more literature about being sick. "Considering how common illness is, how tremendous the spiritual change it brings, how astonishing, when the lights of health go down, the undiscovered countries that are then disclosed . . . what ancient and obdurate oaks are uprooted in us by the act of sickness . . . it becomes strange indeed that illness has not taken its place with love and battle and jealously among the prime themes of literature" (*The Moment and Other Essays,* Harcourt Brace, 1948). Ours is a culture that emphasizes cure, or, short of that, immediate relief from symptoms, so that we can carry on with our busy lives. Unfortunately, in our cultural denial of the reality of chronic illness and disability, we frequently silence the voices of those who cannot deny it.

There's a puzzling myth that people who are ill or injured (especially women) are obsessed with their health—always talking about their problems, showing off their scars, bragging about their doctors. The reality for women with long-term disability or chronic illness is very different, however. Just as we learned at an early age not to acknowledge disability in others ("Don't ask," "Don't stare"), so too we learned not to confront others with our own disabilities—"Don't tell." Unlike the taboos of sex and death, for example, disability and illness have not come into vogue in the popular literature, or in the human potential movement. Part 1 of the book offers works that *do* tell, that reveal the physical and emotional experience of disability and chronic illness.

And there is much to tell. For women who acquire a disability after birth the transition to everyday life is marked by strong and painful emotion, including an often overwhelming sense of loss. The loss of body function becomes a loss of sense of self, as described here in such poems

1

as Murielle Minard's "Affliction" and Nancy Mairs's "Diminishment." The rage or fear that loss can produce are illustrated in the poems "And the True Test Came" by Jo Brooks and "For a Paralyzed Woman Raped and Murdered While Alone in Her Own Apartment" by Leslie A. Donovan. The speaker in Muriel Rukeyser's "Resurrection on the Right Side" attempts, with quiet humor, to reintegrate her loss.

The numerous testimonies in the literature documenting individual triumph over the adversity of physical pain or disease invariably reflect another serious aspect of the oppression of disability: isolation. Unlike members of most other oppressed groups, we are often the only disabled person in the family. Well-meaning friends, family, clergy, and medical caregivers, can offer sympathy and advice, but not that most deeply meaningful, "I know."

This lack of real connection to others is perhaps the greatest pain of disability. "Self-Portrait," a poem by Leslie A. Donovan, expresses the aching sorrow of this isolation; Adrienne Lee Lauby's "Angel Is Sick: Nighttime" reveals our own tendency to protect others from what we are experiencing, thereby increasing our sense of isolation. The narratives, stories, and poems in this part demonstrate there is relief and illumination in the telling, particularly in the telling of these feelings. As Helen Keller has written: "One's life story cannot be told with complete veracity. A true autobiography would have to be written in states of mind, emotions, heartbeats, smiles and tears; not in months and years, or physical events. Life is marked off on the soul-chart by feelings not by dates" (*Midstream: My Later Life,* 1929; rpnt, Greenwood, 1968).

Nevertheless it is not possible to separate the cold facts, the day-to-day reality of living with a disability from the cultural and social obstacles disabled women must face, including outright and indirect discrimination in education and employment. Several works in this part describe the challenges confronting disabled women in the discriminating attitudes of teachers, peers, coworkers, even parents. In "Learning to Work," Dale Brown describes others' unconscious resistance to accommodating to, assisting her with, her learning disability and in "I'm Listening as Hard as I Can," Terry Galloway explores the experience of growing up deaf in a hearing world.

Just as in the larger population, some disabled individuals experience considerable difficulty in their lives; others cope very well, have jobs, and enjoy a full and satisfying life with their friends and families. But the process of adapting or adjusting to a disability can be arduous. In her essay "Pain," Caroline Hardesty discusses her efforts to devise alternative methods of running her household of young children, when arthritis deprives her of movement and flexibility. Barbara Ruth's poem, "In My Disabled Women's Group," describes the need to reorder priorities, goals, life pace. An excerpt from Susan Downer's novel, *Ziante's Time,* reveals the remarkable capacity of humans to overcome obstacles through the metaphor of a young blind Native American girl confronting craggy cliffs and grizzly bears.

Our ability to withstand pain, to heal, and to ask for help in the process, is affected by the perceptions and judgments of those around us, and determines, in part, whether we deny, exaggerate, or overcome our problems. Most disabled people feel that the disability itself, the pain, the need for compensatory devices and assistance can produce considerable inconvenience, but that very often these become minimal or are forgotten once the individual makes the transition to everyday life. But the discriminatory attitudes and thoughtless behaviors, these are what make life difficult, these are the sources of the oppression. The architectural barriers; the pitying stares and frightened avoidance; the unaware assumptions that a disabled woman can't do the job, can't order for herself in a restaurant, can't find a mate or direct her own life, are all symptoms of the problem. The *oppression* is what's disabling about disability.

In the quest to understand the interplay between cultural attitudes and self-perception, the issue of language arises, inevitably and significantly. The correct or "best" terminology to describe disabled people is widely disputed. From times past, we have inherited the words "crippled," "lame," and "handicapped" (thought to have been derived from the beggar's "cap in hand"). In the realms of disability activism, portions of the Midwest accept "handicapped," while the two coasts have begun shunning this descriptor for "disabled." Should we have a new and neutral term for ourselves? The disabled women's movement has generated several, among them: "differently abled," "physically different," "physically challenged," and "other abled."

Some pieces in this section, in the telling of experience, move toward transcending perspectives. Vassar Miller's poem, "Insomniac's Prayer," though about pain, expresses and approaches the desire to be free, to be whole. In "Seal-Woman," a poem by Jo Brooks, we see the imagination play with, deal with limitation.

Different degrees of consciousness, self-acceptance, sophistication (sometimes revealed by or informed by language), reflect our different backgrounds, resources, and myriad influences upon our outlooks. We conclude there is no correct consciousness to strive toward, certainly no endpoint to arrive at. There will always be more to learn, more experiences from others to consider, more growth toward understanding and freedom.

I'm Listening as Hard as I Can

At the age of twelve I won the swimming award at the Lions Camp for Crippled Children. When my name echoed over the PA system the girl in the wheelchair next to me grabbed the box speaker of my hearing aid and shouted, "You won!" My ear quaking, I took the cue. I stood up straight— the only physically unencumbered child in a sea of braces and canes— affixed a pained but brave grin to my face, then limped all the way to the stage.

Later, after the spotlight had dimmed, I was overcome with remorse, but not because I'd played the crippled heroine. The truth was that I was ashamed of my handicap. I wanted to have something more visibly wrong with me. I wanted to be in the same league as the girl who'd lost her right leg in a car accident; her artificial leg attracted a bevy of awestruck campers. I, on the other hand, wore an unwieldy box hearing aid buckled to my body like a dog halter. It attracted no one. Deafness wasn't, in my eyes, a blue-ribbon handicap. Mixed in with my envy, though, was an overwhelming sense of guilt; at camp I was free to splash in the swimming pool, while most of the other children were stranded at the shallow end, where lifeguards floated them in lazy circles. But seventeen years of living in the "normal" world has diminished my guilt considerably, and I've learned that every handicap has its own particular hell.

I'm something of an anomaly in the deaf world. Unlike most deaf people, who were either born deaf or went deaf in infancy, I lost my hearing in chunks over a period of twelve years. Fortunately I learned to speak before my loss grew too profound, and that ability freed me from the most severe problem facing the deaf—the terrible difficulty of making themselves understood. My opinion of deafness was just as biased as that of a person who can hear. I had never met a deaf child in my life, and I didn't know how to sign. I imagined deaf people to be like creatures from beyond: animallike because their language was so physical, threatening because they were unable to express themselves with sophistication—that is, through speech. I *could* make myself understood, and because I had a talent for lipreading it was easy for me to pass in the wider world. And for most of my life that is exactly what I did—like a black woman playing white, I passed for something other than what I was. But in doing so I was avoiding some very painful facts. And for many years I was inhibited not only by my deafness but my own idea of what it meant to be deaf.

My problems all started when my mother, seven months pregnant with me, developed a serious kidney infection. Her doctors pumped her full of antibiotics. Two months later I was born, with nothing to suggest that I was anything more or less than a normal child. For years nobody knew that the antibiotics had played havoc with my fetal nervous system. I grew up bright, happy, and energetic.

But by the time I was ten I knew, if nobody else did, that something somewhere had gone wrong. The people around me had gradually developed fuzzy profiles, and their speech had taken on a blurred and foreign character. But I was such a secure and happy child that it didn't enter my mind to question my new perspective or mention the changes to anyone else. Finally, my behavior became noticeably erratic—I would make nonsensical replies to ordinary questions or simply fail to reply at all. My teachers, deciding that I was neither a particularly creative child nor an especially troublesome one, looked for a physical cause. They found two: I wasn't quite as blind as a bat, but I was almost as deaf as a doornail.

My parents took me to Wilford Hall Air Force Hospital in San Antonio, where I was examined from ear to ear. My tonsils were removed and studied, ice water was injected into my inner ear, and I underwent a series of inexplicable and at times painful exploratory tests. I would forever after associate deafness with kind attention and unusual punishment. Finally a verdict was delivered: "Congenital interference has resulted in a neural disorder for which there is no known medical or surgical treatment." My hearing loss was severe and would grow progressively worse.

I was fitted with my first hearing aid and sent back home to resume my childhood. I never did. I had just turned twelve, and my body was undergoing enormous changes. I had baby fat, baby breasts, hairy legs, and thick pink cat-eye glasses. My hearing aid was about the size of a small transistor radio and rode in a white linen pouch that hit exactly at breast level. It was not a welcome addition to my pubescent woe.

As a vain child trapped in a monster's body, I was frantic for a way to survive the next few years. Glimpsing my reflection in mirrors became such agony that I acquired a habit of brushing my teeth and hair with my eyes closed. Everything I did was geared to making my body more inhabitable, but I only succeeded in making it less so. I kept my glasses in my pocket and developed an unbecoming squint; I devised a smile that hid two broken front teeth, but it looked disturbingly like the grin of a piranha; I kept my arms folded over my would-be breasts. But the hearing aid was a different story. There was no way to disguise it. I could tuck it under my blouse, but then all I could hear was the static of cotton. Besides, whenever I took a step the box bounced around like a third breast. So I resigned myself: a monster I was, a monster I would be.

I became more withdrawn, more suspicious of other people's intentions. I imagined that I was being deliberately excluded from schoolyard talk because the other children didn't make much of an effort to involve me—they simply didn't have the time or patience to repeat snatches of gossip ten times and slowly. Conversation always reached the point of ridiculousness before I could understand something as simple as "The movie starts at five." (The groovy shark's alive? The moving stars that thrive?) I didn't make it to many movies. I cultivated a lofty sense of superiority, and I was often brutal with people who offered the "wrong" kind of help at the "wrong" time. Right after my thirteenth birthday some well-meaning neighbors took me to a revivalist faith healing. I already had doubts about exuberant religions, and the knee-deep hysteria of the preacher simply confirmed them. He bounded to my side and put his hands on my head. "O Lord," he cried, "heal this poor little lamb!"

I leaped up as if transported and shouted, "I can walk!"

For the first few years my parents were as bewildered as I was. Nothing had prepared them for a handicapped child on the brink of adolescence. They sensed a whole other world of problems, but in those early stages I still seemed so normal that they just couldn't see me in a school for the deaf. They felt that although such schools were there to help, they also served to isolate. I have always been grateful for their decision. Because of it, I had to contend with public schools, and in doing so I developed two methods of survival: I learned to read not just lips but the whole person, and I learned the habit of clear speech by taking every speech and drama course I could.

That is not to say my adolescent years were easy going—they were misery. The lack of sound cast a pall on everything. Life seemed less fun than it had been before. I didn't associate that lack of fun with the lack of sound. I didn't begin to make the connection between the failings of my body and the failings of the world until I was well out of college. I simply did not admit to myself that deafness caused certain problems—or even that I was deaf.

From the time I was twelve until I was twenty-four, the loss of my hearing was erratic. I would lose a decibel or two of sound and then my hearing would stabilize. A week or a year later there would be another slip and then I'd have to adjust all over again. I never knew when I would hit bottom. I remember going to bed one night still being able to make out the reassuring purr of the refrigerator and the late-night conversation of my parents, then waking the next morning to nothing—even my own voice was gone. These fits and starts continued until my hearing finally dropped to the last rung of amplifiable sound. I was a college student at the time, and whenever anyone asked about my hearing aid, I admitted to being only slightly hard of hearing.

My professors were frequently alarmed by my almost maniacal intensity in class. I was petrified that I'd have to ask for special privileges just to achieve marginal understanding. My pride was in flames. I became increasingly bitter and isolated. I was terrified of being marked a deaf woman, a label that made me sound dumb and cowlike, enveloped in a protective silence that denied me my complexity. I did everything I could to hide my handicap. I wore my hair long and never wore earrings, thus keeping attention away from my ears and their riders. I monopolized conversations so that I wouldn't slip up and reveal what I was or wasn't hearing; I took on a disdainful air at large parties, hoping that no one would ask me something I couldn't instantly reply to. I lied about the extent of my deafness so I could avoid the stigma of being thought "different" in a pathetic way.

It was not surprising that in my senior year I suffered a nervous collapse and spent three days in the hospital crying like a baby. When I stopped crying I knew it was time to face a few things—I had to start asking for help when I needed it because I couldn't handle my deafness alone, and I had to quite being ashamed of my handicap so I could begin to live with its consequences and discover what (if any) were its rewards.

When I began telling people that I was *really* deaf I did so with grim determination. Some were afraid to talk to me at any length, fearing perhaps that they were talking into a void; others assumed that I was somehow an unsullied innocent and always inquired in carefully enunciated sentences; "Dooooooo youuuuuuuu driiinnk liquor?" But most people were surprisingly sympathetic—they wanted to know the best way to be understood, they took great pains to talk directly to my face, and they didn't insult me by using only words of one syllable.

It was, in part, that gentle acceptance that made me more curious about my own deafness. Always before it had been an affliction to wrestle with as one would with angels, but when I finally accepted it as an inevitable part of my life, I relaxed enough to do some exploring. I would take off my hearing aid and go through a day, a night, an hour or two—as long as I could take it—in absolute silence. I felt as if I were indulging in a secret vice because I was perceiving the world in a new way—stripped of sound.

Of course I had always known that sound is vibration, but I didn't know, until I stopped straining to hear, how truly sound is a refinement of feeling. Conversations at parties might elude me, but I seldom fail to pick up on moods. I enjoy watching people talk. When I am too far away to read lips I try reading postures and imagining conversations. Sometimes, to everyone's horror, I respond to things better left unsaid when I'm trying to find out what's going on around me. I want to see, touch, taste, and smell everything within reach; I especially have to curb a tendency to judge things by their smell—not just potato salad but people as well—a habit that seems to some people entirely too barbaric for comfort. I am not claiming that my other senses stepped up their work to compensate for the loss, but the absence of one does allow me to concentrate on the others. Deafness has left me acutely aware of both the duplicity that language is capable of and the many expressions the body cannot hide.

Nine years ago I spent the summer at the University of Texas' experimental Shakespeare workshop at Winedale, and I went back each year for eight years, first as a student and then as a staff associate. Off and on for the last four years I have written and performed for Esther's Follies, a cabaret theater group in Austin. Some people think it's odd that, as deaf as I am, I've spent so much of my life working in the theater, but I find it to be a natural consequence of my particular circumstance. The loss of sound has enhanced my fascination with language and the way meaning is conveyed. I love to perform. Exactly the same processes occur onstage as off—except that onstage, once I've memorized the script, I know what everybody is saying as they say it. I am delighted to be so immediately in the know. It has provided a direct way to keep in touch with the rest of the world despite the imposed isolation.

Silence is not empty; it is simply more sobering than sound. At times I prefer the sobriety. I can still "hear" with a hearing aid—that is, I can discern noise, but I can't tell you where it's coming from or if it is laughter or a faulty drain. When there are many people talking together I hear a strange music, a distant rumbling in my consciousness. But when I take off my hearing aid at night and lie in bed surrounded by my fate, I wonder, "What is this—a foul subtraction or a blessing in disguise?" For despite my fears there is a kind of peace in the silence—albeit an uneasy one. There is, after all, less to distract me from my thoughts.

But I know what I've lost. The process of becoming deaf has at times been frightening, akin perhaps to dying, and early in life it took away my happy confidence in the image of a world where things always work right. When I first came back from the Lions Camp that summer I cursed heaven and earth for doing such terrible wrong to me and to my friends. My grandmother tried to comfort me by promising, "Honey, God's got something special planned for you."

But I thought, "Yes. He plans to make me deaf."

Murielle Minard

Affliction

Affliction
Is ice
On a summer pond.
And the pond
Not dead,
But subtly robbed
Of pondness.

Carolyn S. Foote

Arthritis

Nine fingers stride
across the keyboard
with acceptable skill;
the tenth's a laggard.

There's no chance it will
catch up.

Bach and Buxtehude
flinch in old graves
where my dismal, crooked digit
belongs also.

I'd like to abandon it
on someone's doorsill.

from Ziante's Time

In the days when life was all Ohloni, and talk of strangers in winged canoes was but one more strand of web in all stories, Rima Teressa, then known simply as Rima, was born to the antelope lineage on a tributary of an inland creek—and she was born blind. Her grandmother (also the shaman) took Rima south to where Ziante's river ran most crookedly, and hid her in a canyon there and raised her like a young animal, trying always to open her eyes.

It took the grandmother considerable time to gauge the severity of Rima's blindness as well as the differences it made in her growth and play. She was definitely drawn toward light, her eyes seeming almost to flicker at times with the crazy sputter of fire on the hearth. For a short while after her birth, she seemed aware of colors too, staring fixedly at the beige lines in Grandmother's buckskin skirt or darting first eyes and then hands toward a winking periwinkle in Grandmother's shell necklace. Gradually, however, these behaviors ceased.

Unlike other babies whom Grandmother had known, Rima never prattled when she heard a step or voice approach her. She must be silent, Grandmother reasoned, in order to hear that which came near. Vision, the usual distance sense, had been deprived her. Unless she heard, smelt, touched, or tasted something, it didn't exist for her. Therefore it was left to Grandmother to see for Rima, and through words, provide all that eyes would ordinarily provide. "Hear the pot spitting on the fire? That means supper's on." Or, "Too many scratching noises in our walls, Rima. Insects are eating our tule nest again. We'll have to pull that part down and weave another."

Rima first sensed the world through her skin, which itched pleasantly in places where it rubbed against her grass mattress, and hurt where constrained by hemp rope to a cradleboard. She learned to distinguish day from night by listening. Morning always started with the "chink" of the brown towhee and the high burble of quail, then the rachet voice of raven, the chortling of grosbeak, and the three-noted "whip-three-dee" of olive-sided flycatcher. Around flycatcher time Grandmother would rustle beside Rima in her deerskin bedclothes, roll over on her back and sleep a little longer, her mouth open, her breath escaping in furtive gusts, rattling and dry. Sometimes Grandmother snored too, drowning out even the boisterous scrub jays until a particularly sharp breath caught in her throat and startled her awake. Exuberantly then, she would fan away her quilt, and seconds later, just beyond their tule nest, Rima would hear Grandmother's low, rippling incantation of praise to sunrise; a whimsical song, half muffled and pigeon-throated, half brilliant, like meadowlark. Like light itself, Rima supposed! If there were fog or rain clouds, the song hovered and coaxed, and when the rain actually poured, dampening the scent of their tule roof, then Grandmother mightn't sing at all and the two of them would sleep late. The next sound after sun praise was usually fire snapping in the pit beside Rima's cradleboard, fire which always teased her nose with its curious mixture of woodsmoke, pitch of redwood needles, berry juice, and frying meat.

Later, if the day was warm, Grandmother would bathe Rima in the crooked river and afterward play with her under the chestnut and oak trees, rolling her about in the scratchy grass and then caressing the bones of her face and scalp in a manner that, because of Grandmother's strength and the rough calluses on her palms, both hurt and soothed Rima. It was a loving sort of hurt, and by degrees it pressed her bones into the flat, smooth features of a true Ohloni. Grandmother explained that every mother molded her child's face in this manner, but that she must sculpt Rima with extra zeal, because the more Rima looked and acted Ohloni, the more likely it was that her senses would serve her fully as an Ohloni's senses must.

Rima's first memories were like those of a young animal, fragmented and inborn: Grandmother's coarse hand laid in hers (that hand that felt like serrated pieces of abalone shell); a raccoon kit, Tctoiiwewa, whose shaggy body and paws seemed always wet whenever he scrambled on or off Rima's lap; a scent of wild azalea; a time when the crooked river leapt its banks and filled their canyon to its rim, so that their nest floated among the trees, and both day and night roared with wind and water.

She maneuvered on her hands and knees through every cranny of the canyon, learning as a snake learns, through her skin, discerning not only texture, but also time notions (before, after) and distance notions (near, far). She knew by the intensity of the sun's heat which day and season were passing in her canyon. And she listened, always listened on its rims, for voices from the outside. Once, drowsing in the sun:

"Grandmother?"

"What is it, daughter?"

"What's the rustle on the grass?"

"I hear nothing, child."

"Yes you do, below the laurel trees."

"It's the sound of the legs of women passing with burden baskets."

"The grass rattles like a snake, Grandmother. What are they doing?"

"They are beating the broom grasses with sticks to harvest seed. You hear the daughter? She is talking to the path so it will not trip them."

"Let me pass you. I'm going to meet them."

"You are not! Lie down in the gully at once so they won't see you."

"What will they do with their seed?"

"Share it with many families. They will burn the meadow too. You will smell it tonight or tomorrow."

"Why will they burn it?"

"So the ash can feed the ground and make their seed come again next year."

"And why must they share it with other families?"

"Because if they do not, then others become jealous, and their jealousy poisons the seed meadow so that nothing will grow."

"Grandmother, let me touch them!"

"You will never touch them."

That word "never" was all right for the moment, but the following morning Grandmother dismantled their tule nest and led them on a meandering day's journey to yet another canyon, where, she vowed, they'd not be stumbled upon by stragglers seeking a seed meadow. As Rima grew older, Grandmother said "never," "don't," and "stop" all too frequently, and where her companionship had once been Rima's eye on the world, it now seemed to shield her, blotting life out the way water did when it covered her ears and nose.

Yet there was something worse than Grandmother's stealthy protection of her; that something was Grandmother's shaman journeys. She began making them during Rima's twelfth year when Matelian, the great shaman who replaced her after Rima's birth, died. Often she was absent for an entire season. With only the whooshing, tattering, voice-conjuring wind for company, Rima found the adamant, self-nurturing efficiency that was her core, and the yearning for a loved one, Anyone—a yearning she would retain as her closest companion long after many loved ones (husband, sister, children) had crowded her life.

The first quail sounded and Rima struck at morning like a cornered rattlesnake, springing from sleep so rapidly she made herself dizzy and rushing to the river for her morning bath. The water was icy, setting her already frayed, razor-grass nerves even more on edge. Serviceberries ripened on the riverbank, and Rima tore a handful from the bush and devoured them, not minding that the hard sours were mixed in with the sweet. Then she shook some broom grass seeds loose from a basket of stems she had gathered the night before and ate those also. She tasted neither fruit nor seeds. In part she ate from panic, because eating was one more motion that kept her from listening to a canyon empty of Grandmother's sleep snores.

The rabbit snares were empty again. That was Rima's own fault for allowing the top layer of brush to sift down through the trapdoor of branches. The brush mound inside each snare had grown so high that even the smallest cottontail could climb out. She would eat no meat again tonight, unless she happened to catch a pocket gopher.

A sandy chafe of teeth and insect wings assailed her ears as she re-entered her nest. She groped carefully along the tule walls until she found the hairy moth bodies and crisp locusts. They had eaten so much where the rear wall joined the roof that a piece of ceiling thatch had fallen. Had she only picked the insects loose every day, this never would have happened. Indeed, she could only recall its happening twice in all the time Grandmother lived with her. Now there was nothing left but to gather deer grass and willow greens from the river and weave a new section of roof to replace that which she'd neglected. The wall would probably have to come down too. That meant finding, uprooting, and stripping new willow poles. Everything about the job would be difficult without Grandmother. There was scarcely any deer grass growing in their own canyon, so Rima would have to venture onto unfamiliar land, remaining mindful of earth heaves, boulders, and tree roots that she could use. as clues to guide herself back home. If she were fortunate enough not to get lost, she might still come home empty-handed, because this was summer, when nearly all grasses withered, too brittle for use. If she found fresh grass and willow, there was still the arduous task of weaving, hoisting, and stretching so huge a section of thatch without aid. Wearily she sighed and set to.

Noontime droned with flies and ants. Rima had scaled the west canyon wall and near its rim found a few unexpected greens. Her arms were already weary of the harvest, and her throat felt doubly parched from thirst and the astringency of air redolent of pine sap and limestone dust.

A thick, wet-nostrilled snuffle startled her, followed by a dark, airless thud of paws that sounded as though layers of earth were picking themselves up and walking. Grizzly! Remaining on all fours, she scooted carefully backward down the same western wall she'd just clambered up, feeling all the while for a pit between the rocks in which she might hide. The snuffling noise grew louder. Near ground level, an actual cistern in the rocks availed itself. Without pausing to kick a stone down ahead of her to learn the hole's depth, Rima held her breath and plunged.

Rainwater and a veritable bog of decaying bay leaves cushioned her fall. She'd broken no bones, and she'd not likely meet a rattlesnake in a swamp as wet as this one. From above, the grizzly's snuffle came even nearer. He sounded tall and heavy. Suppose he had already picked up her scent, and suppose her hiding pit wasn't deep or narrow enough to scare him off? Suppose he could climb down into the pit with her while still keeping his head and forepaws above ground? She longed to feel with her hand for the top of her enclosure but she dared not.

The ground above her sobbed and sucked. The bear sneezed, groaned, and pushed something (a rock or a sapling) so that it cracked sharply. Then he was silent except for his wet snuffle, rhythmic now instead of erratic. He wasn't moving on then! He intended to stay there! What should she do? Not stir, certainly, for his wet nose might at that very instant be leaning on the edge of her hideaway. Even now he might be watching her, readying himself to spring.

The hairs on Rima's legs twitched. Feet were crawling, pincering their way beneath her buckskin skirt. She shuddered. Spiders! In this swamp they were probably not the furry, mint-plant variety either, but tarantulas. Three times during her twelve years they had bitten her, and each bite had caused a high fever. Grandmother had warned her to beware of them if she ever hid in damp places. She mustn't swat them; they would crawl from her of their own accord.

So she lay motionless as did her enemy above, while the tiny enemies into whose lair she had tumbled swarmed over her body. Their feet made her itch and break into a cold sweat. Some of them even mouthed her skin and she feared that at any instant, one would bite and draw her blood. Then, too, the wet bog was soaking her. She began to shiver and to stifle sneezes so that the bear mightn't hear her. If only Grandmother were near! Grandmother would have hidden her in a drier place. Perhaps Grandmother would have killed the bear with an arrow, or charmed it with the shaman's yanna tobacco, the herb that only fully entrusted healers were allowed to gather. Hiding had been Rima's only recourse.

Panic began wheedling away at Rima, the way a mouse wheedles a cluster of coffee berries. Suppose nightfall arrived and the bear still waited above her. Suppose she spent the night in this bog, took cold in her lungs, and died. She imagined herself moldering away, a meal for termites and spiders, imagined Grandmother returning from her long journey of shaman rounds, and calling Rima's name but hearing no reply. Searching, searching, Grandmother might even find this bog and peer down into it, but by that time there would be nothing left of Rima except some telltale scrap of skirt.

Suddenly the bear uttered a half grumble, half snort, rustled the immediate brush, and began a slow retreat. Rima waited until she no longer heard him. Then, carefully she stirred her legs, on which no spiders had crawled for some time now. Nothing in the bog moved. Violently she shook the matted leafage around her so that it cheeped and lisped. Still no spiders. She scrambled to her knees and groped about the wet prison. Its walls were steep and slimy and for an instant she thought she might have maneuvered her own watery suicide. But then her fingers closed around spikes and loops of tree root, zigzagging their way up one side of the pit and, if she proceeded cautiously, affording her a treacherous escape.

She was exhausted by the time she'd worked her way back home. She didn't even bother to retrieve what little grass she'd harvested that morning, but left the task to some day in the vague future. The steep tilt of sunlight told her it was now late afternoon, but there was still plenty of heat in which to dry herself.

Uneasily she stretched out on the ground in front of her door. Was danger over for that day? What if a bobcat came, stalking so silently that only the musky odor of its fur warned Rima of its presence? Or what if a pack of coyotes found her after sundown where she sat in her tule hole, now open to the night through its roof and on one side? Her fire would prevent their attacking her, and a handful of pebbles tossed in their direction would probably make them tuck their tails between their legs. Still, the thought of them yipping near her in the darkness, with nothing but sky between them and herself, made her dreadfully uncomfortable. Torturing herself with these worries and a yearning for Grandmother, Rima fell unhappily asleep.

Nancy Mairs ———————————————————

Diminishment

My body
is going away.

It fades
to the transparency
of rubbed amber
held against the sun.

It shrinks.
It grows quiet.

Small, quiet,
it is a cold
and heavy
smoothed stone.

Who will have it
when it lies
pale and polished
as a clean bone?

And the True Test Came

Natural rose
hips
and your lips kiss
soft and surgary
the real thing
not artificial cancer-causing
substitutes
as hard and tight
as the cap on a bottle
of sedatives . . .

after my body
changed into a stranger
one, scars meant scary
bony meant bad
scared meant run
and I was getting smaller
in the distance
between us—
I was kept in my place
which was not
near you—
you changed too
as time told the truth
that I was new
and never again

rage grew too
remembering
pine tree forests
and beds of violets
where we walked
together hands held
heads held where our eyes
pretty much meeting
looked deeper melting
into our own violet souls
as we made love

cries
on a mountain top
inaccessible
forever after

and the true test
came to dreams
that the future
sat in front of campfires
of inexhaustible driftwood
in the backwood nights
of Maine
or crawled along the sand
where only seabirds protected
their young and an infinity
of gemstones—
at sunset, smiling—on any cape
when the nightmare
glared in the sun
rise

and I sit
forever after
inaccessible
to the sheep
of Wales and the Appalachian
trails never traveled
together with my natural
lips scarred
and hard
and my soft sugared
hips numb
held
in the distant memory
wilderness just at dusk
hearing the lone coyote's
cry
blend into my own
disappearing . . .

Pain

I used to be a seeker of pain. Every weekday morning, a friend and I swapped our young daughters while we took turns running—just a mile or two. The prospect of strong slim thighs made the muscular sting pleasurable.

But about five months into our routine, I developed a pain that wasn't from hard-working muscles. The balls of my feet were stiff and objected to the pressure of my weight. I blamed the rough ice of January roads and the fact that I ran in an old pair of tennis shoes. And I ignored it. Some days it was slight in one foot and distracting in the other. Or it was worst when I stepped out of bed but tolerable for running a short time later.

Then one morning, about two blocks into my jog, the pain won. Whatever the cause, this daily abuse wasn't helping.

Ending the morning runs did little if anything to dissipate the pain, yet I thought the irritation would in time take care of itself. I had rarely been sick and illnesses usually took a short cycle and disappeared without medical advice. Instead of leaving, though, the symptoms wandered to other joints. As summer began, my ankles and knees hurt and I had trouble rising from chairs. My walk became somewhat stiff. Then the discomfort moved into my shoulders, elbows, and hands, but never as a bright searing pain. Some days, in fact, it was barely noticeable and I proceeded with life as if I had a hangnail. Those days reinforced my belief that whatever it was, it was going away.

Refusing to be hampered, I volunteered to be in charge of painting the backdrop for our community's first summer musical. And still seeking the strong body-beautiful a thirty-two-year-old woman should have, I frequently exercised at the swimming pool, where the buoying water relieved my joints and the bottoms of my feet. And I doggedly ate little. By August, I'd lost about twenty pounds along with the ability to see any gauntness in my 110 pound, nearly five foot eight-inch frame.

And the pain—from nagging aches up and down my tendons to sharp and unpredictable pings or PINGS like sudden fireworks bursting in and around my joints—was constant; I finally went to a doctor.

He interviewed me briefly, had me grip his fingers in my clenched fists, gave me a blood sedimentation test, and told me I had palindromic rheumatoid arthritis, a type that cripples you one day and overlooks you the next. His generous drug samples were my first medicinal intrusions. Unfortunately they made it worse. Where formerly one or two joints troubled me on any specific day, the chemicals seemed to generalize it; all joints began to hurt.

I tried one drug after another as autumn spread, but the pain increased. It hurt to move, and eventually, it hurt without any movement at all.

I began learning about this condition, which I couldn't help but associate with the aging housekeeper in the Bobbsey Twins series who complained from time to time about her " 'tiz." What I found was that, despite its association with the disease that affects the calcium-starved bones of older women, rheumatoid arthritis strikes mostly young and middle-aged women between the ages of eighteen and fifty. Over seven million in this country are afflicted.

At my mother's urging, I sought further help from the specialists at nearby University of Iowa Hospital. The doctors there said: "The cheapest medicine for you is aspirin and it would probably do you as much good as clinirol (my then current and favored drug). We don't know if you'll improve, or if so when.

"From the severity of your case, we would recommend gold treatments. The gold has a cumulative effect and you'll need injections weekly. After ten weeks, we'll know if you're reacting favorably. But you'll have to watch for side effects, especially any kind of skin rash. Call us immediately if that happens."

A skin rash meant interior problems, one of which was kidney damage. The doctors had no answers to my questions about diet, my saltless tears, or the putrid odor of my urine. I wasn't pleased with the risks of gold, not to mention the costs (a sister-in-law asked, "Couldn't you just suck on your wedding ring?"). Our extensive medical insurance did not cover expenses for a disease such as arthritis.

I turned to aspirin—up to twenty-five grains per day. I couldn't sleep unless I was more tired than pained. Waking in the night to pop more pills, I lay awake waiting again to be more weary than hurt.

That winter, 1980–81, was a season of hell for me. I was never warm enough, but the weight of extra clothing or blankets hurt. I couldn't sit on the floor because with sore, unbending wrists, I couldn't get up. (My main reason for wanting to be on the floor was my two-year-old.) Despite the admonishments of my mother, who thought the warm water would be a comfort, I gave up baths: I couldn't bear the humiliation of having someone lift me out of the tub and the logistics seemed insurmountable since I couldn't tolerate any kind of pulling at my wrists, elbows, or shoulders.

Sometimes I walked—shuffled, really—with a cane to assist my aching knees and stiff, pained, elephantine ankles. Occasionally my silly toddler took the cane, humped over, and "walked like Mom." I laughed to tears.

Where once I prided myself on efficiently unloading the dishwasher by grasping four dinner plates simultaneously in one hand, I had to move to

the monkey-minded version of two hands for one plate, boosting it nois-
ily onto the stack in the cupboard; plastic held more appeal than ever
before. If I wanted ice, I had to leave the tray at room temperature for
awhile: I was unable to flex the plastic holder enough to loosen frozen
cubes.

My dearest aunt sent me an electric can opener since I could not grip the
handles of a manual one with enough force to puncture a lid. We switched
from cloth to paper diapers because I couldn't open or shut a safety pin. I
struggled with embarrassment when I scrawled a check at the grocery
store, where the clerks must have had a secret code for their carry-out
assistants who toted my single bag to the car without even asking. I made
a rare visit to a hair salon for a permanent so my hair would take care of
itself after a quick shampoo in the shower (this I could do only by easing
my arms up, never elbows out).

Cooking was laborious but I stubbornly clung to the ritual, refusing to
adopt fast-food meals. My twelve-year-old helped when I asked and enter-
tained me with her junior high life. Though I know how much it hurt her
to see me so handicapped, she cheered me on with after-school greetings
like, "Hi, Crip, how's it going?" It was our way of denying the disease its
power to control. My husband, who had always been a more assiduous
cleaner than I, did more. He also helped me dress and undress.

I lived my days slowly, creating methods to maintain independence in
necessary routines. I couldn't squeeze toothpaste with my hand so I held
the tube between the sink and my hip and leaned on it. I had to use both
hands, in a cross-leverage fashion, to brush my teeth. I braced myself with
the sink and wall when I used the toilet. To lift my child into her high-
chair, I hoisted her under her armpits with the middles of my forearms.
Sweeping her up for a hug was out of the question; the only way we
exchanged those was when she crawled onto my lap, and even then I
couldn't embrace her as I wanted.

For a time it hurt to move my jaw, and the weight of the fork, uncomfortable on its own, increased perceptibly when I added food to it. I ate
less. For evening distractions, I read—but only paperbacks. Balancing
hardbound books was too painful. Imprisoned in a diseased body determined to keep me from normal life, I felt frustration and anger as well as
pain and weariness. A lot of the time I wanted to die.

Countering that fatalism were the concerns of all the people who cared
about me. Family and friends in and out of town expressed their love in
very generous ways. My former running partner was a constant and patient source of friendship, dropping in for visits, and often taking my little
girl with her when she ran errands.

Another line of hope was through a woman whose history made my
problems seem manageable. She had had juvenile rheumatoid arthritis
that had gone into remission, and then in adulthood, returned. Her trials

included surgery on both hands while she had a preschooler and an infant to care for. Gretchen brought me absorbing books by British novelists Margaret Drabble and Barbara Pym, and she brought catalogs of down clothing and advice on things like shoes (supportive shoes with wool socks were much better for walking than the warm down slippers my hopeful parents had given me). And her presence repeatedly brought me the vision of possibilities. Her sometimes stiff walk and impaired hands revealed the disease in her own life, but she was a part-time graduate student and a stringer for an area newspaper. She was functioning, and her existence and encouragement brought me hope.

On the advice of another friend, I applied aloe vera cream to my feet, and from an article sent by my mother, I quit eating wheat—not an easy sacrifice because I loved it. And day by day, I believed I finally wasn't getting worse.

On February 13, almost a year after I'd quit running, my older daughter sprained her ankle, and on the way to the X-ray room, the young, nutrition-minded general practitioner asked me why I was limping. I took the chance to ask again about diet and its relation to arthritis. He said no substantial links had ever been found, and I wondered about my self-healing methods. Just coincidence?

I celebrated his words the next day by baking heart-shaped cookies and engaging in a favorite vice of snitching cookie dough. That evening we went with friends to an exhibition tennis match where I had my own Valentine Day's massacre. As the games were finishing, I felt blasts of heat in my joints. I concentrated hard on the way to the car to move my legs forward, to move them at all. At home, I burst into tears. My body was on fire. My husband undressed me—a routine I had resumed—and I lay in bed imagining the Olympic torch runner fleeting from joint to joint, lighting each on fire, over and over.

I've never gone back to a doctor for advice on my condition. I didn't want to take gold, so my treatment was confined to aspirin and whichever amateur method I chose. (Receiving such discouraging advice from the medical community from whom we tend to expect miracles anyway, I became very sympathetic with people who are suckered into trying so-called quack reliefs. In pain and desperation, what may sound like outrageous solutions become causes for hope. And sometimes they *do* work, whether because of the placebo effect or because of some personal idiosyncracy.) From that point on, I relied on hearsay and books, period. Alfalfa tablets from the Shaklee woman, vitamin C from Norman Cousin's *Anatomy of an Illness*, aloe vera drink, purified water, cod liver oil from my mother, and no more wheat.

Some of my reading led me to try a fast. For three days I drank only water and each day I felt noticeably better. I continued concocting breads out of rice flour or other recipe inventions given me by family and friends, and resisted the aromatic whole wheat loaves that I stubbornly, and finally with the help of a food processor, baked for my family. Some months later I fasted another three days and while I was actively avoiding food, I forgot to take aspirin. The pain had decreased enough by then so that I slept through the night. After the fast, the pain was in tolerable limits. I knew where I hurt and acted accordingly. Since that time, I've taken probably fewer than what once comprised a day's dosage.

Improvement is slow and uneven. Seasonal activities seem easier every year—raking leaves, pulling my now six-year-old on her sled (done with the rope around my chest, not towing with one hand), digging in the garden, playing the piano, even taking peaceful, short bike rides. And I can sit on the floor again. Not with grace, but I can do it. Last year, urged on by my young daughter for a short sprint, I ran as though I wore casts on both legs. This year I can run a respectable block. Some days. It will never be sport for me again.

And I can use my hands once more. I forget about the swollen and distorted knuckles until I suddenly catch myself in a mirror or see them in a photograph. I don't like the way they look, but as with my slightly crowded teeth I forget to be delicate about them, forget to hold them in a position that makes them appear more normal. That they function is what matters.

I don't expect complete remission; that old dream of waking to smooth joints and a painfree body disappeared years ago. But I've learned how to live with the condition and I imagine myself perfectly capable of surviving well. The moments I still feel raw anger are those when I battle unforgiving mechanical objects—lifting a springless Volvo trunk lid, squeezing a gas pump handle, fighting a screw that won't budge. Those things remind me of helplessness and they raise a rage. I hate asking for help.

And sometimes I feel an ache coming on that I know will wake me in the night and send me downstairs to prop myself up on the couch with ice bags and a book. But it's been a blessedly long time since that's happened.

The most frustrating thing about unwelcome and chronic pain is its mandate to revise your life. Revision marks a measure of acceptance. And to accept it feels too much like abandoning independence.

Despite occasional struggles, my body and I have reached a level of agreement, one that doesn't seem so much abandonment as compromise. And when I consider the contrast between the time of hopelessness and my growing abilities to proceed with life despite the condition, I make those compromises gratefully.

Resurrection of the Right Side

When the half-body dies its frightful death
forked pain, infection of snakes, lightning, pull down the
    voice. Waking
and I begin to climb the mountain on my mouth,
word by stammer, walk stammered, the lurching deck of
    earth.
Left-right with none of my own rhythms
the long-established sex and poetry.
                            I go running in sleep,
but waking stumble down corridors of self, all rhythms
    gone.

The broken movement of love   sex out of rhythm
one halted name   in a shattered language
ruin of French-blue lights behind the eyes
slowly the left hand extends a hundred feet
and the right hand follows follows
but still the power of sight is very weak
but I go rolling this ball of life, it rolls
and I follow it whole up the slowly-brightening slope

A whisper attempts me, I whisper without stammer
I walk the long hall to the time of a metronome
set by a child's gun-target   left-right
the power of eyesight is very slowly arriving
        in this late impossible daybreak
        all the blue flowers open

Angel Is Sick: Nighttime

Shit: snakes floating, some worms, gray-green, probably strong smell. *Asthma:* kept down by meds, machine, and very clean room. *Guts:* some tenderness and pain, allowable. *Tongue:* raw. *Nose:* congested, occasionally air through one nostril. *Mind:* strong, clear, tendencies to repetition. *Emotions:* sad, lonely, calm, rested, afraid for the night ahead. *Time:* 9 P.M.

Midnight. Had she slept? Yes, she could remember dreaming. First the red, yellow, and orange turtle who was so wise; then, measuring tongues with another woman. So nice. Good. There's feeling in here somewhere. Okay, now what? Why was she awake?

Angel turned on the light and felt her stomach move, wide open bubbles. Her stomach was keeping her up; that's right, the dream images had been more like fantasy because her stomach wouldn't let her go far enough away to dream. She'd known this would happen. That's why she had stayed up late tonight (most nights), writing a letter that would not be sent until this phase of acute symptoms had gone. No sense upsetting someone too far away to help, too guilty not to worry, and too tired ever to want to help again. Mom. Then, the discovery of a way to read her book, covering the pages with glass from an old picture frame. A wonderful way to keep the ink (or was it the paper?) from reaching her nose. Tonight she'd even carried the book to the toilet with her, first time for that—the glass could cut bad if dropped and you fell, if chipped against the wall and bumped across your stomach. Soon, sometime, she'd get a sheet of plexiglass but for now it was a miracle to read. Just that. To have an interest for her mind outside her body; five feet, seven inches of upright bone. Such a small ghetto.

A throat tickle and Angel remembered the rest. The coughing followed the tickle and soon she'd be sick. Which came first tonight? The tickle or the gut? Both followed exposure to something. But what? At the desk, her legs covered with a robe, she wondered how many times she'd poured medication into the plastic cup of the air machine. How often wondered if the hose and valves were clean enough, sterile; taken the tooth-scarred mouthpiece toward her tongue wondering if her lungs would be hurt or helped? Wondering if the medicine for the asthma hadn't caused the diarrhea, hadn't caused these sudden reactions to the natural and unnatural. She leaned close and hit the switch. Loneliness.

Even though Gail had told her several times to call ("I've called you in the middle of the night a lot. You could do it now and then when you need to"), she would not call Gail tonight. Gail might be sleeping with Karen and she was too sick to deal with the possibility of that ringing phone. Three more days and the weekend would end. Five more days and she'd see Gail. Their regular date. As usual when the attacks started, her bladder muscles went soggy. She flipped the switch closed and squatted over her thrift store pitcher to pee. Nothing much. She hadn't drank enough today. Or done her vitamins. Or planned food for tomorrow. Or called Vickie for help this weekend. She hadn't hadn't done done. She hadn't looked at next week to see what she would cancel. The air, switched again to a steady breathing rhythm, seemed to help. No one could say why a caffeine-type drug intended to stimulate bronchial tubes worked against an allergy tickle. It did sometimes. Sometimes it didn't. Maybe tonight it would.

Her nose popped and she blew out one side. Good. Felt clear, felt like it would never be clogged again. Hope and joy broke from her shaking fingers like rugs beaten free in the spring; (the drugs!) the drugs that made her fingers tremble could heal this nose. Her nostril cemented again. Oh, yes. She needed to drink more water. As she waited for the tap to run warm (amazing to have a sink in her bedroom—this house was special for sick people), she turned on the overhead light. Better to pretend it was still day. There'd been enough soft romantic miserable lamplight to last ten years. Sick and alone was not romance. Sick and alone was a practical work ethic day.

Her slippers trailed on the freshly mopped floor, the bed still almost neat with clean bedding. Maybe she wasn't allergic to dust, mold, cat dander; maybe it was like the sugar pills they gave, deluding you to health. But she didn't mind a delusion if it worked and felt safer in her room since Almond had stayed an extra day to deal with it. Friendship was not to be sneezed at and also she could feel sad and lonely. After all Almond was down the hall sleeping and driving two states away tomorrow. Sick and alone. Sick was being alone. She grabbed the doorknob and headed for the toilet. This was one shit that would not wait politely. Was that good? Had the water caused it to explode?

An hour later. You call this an hour? Felt more like sixty minutes, if sixty minutes was a feeling of six ten-minute failures to sleep. She'd been doing pursed-lip breathing and adding tighten-relax muscle pulls on her exhale. Stress reduction, they called it now, professional experts mixing techniques she'd learned years ago in yoga workouts for free. Deep breath in, release slowly through whistle-shaped mouth, softly, silently; tighten toes for exhale, release suddenly on inhale; exhale, tighten ankles and lower calves. Tighten tighten tighten tighten. Release. Until every muscle had been separated and used, until ten separate six minutes passed and she was not stress reduced. She was afraid. Still early and this breath pulled from her lungs with a sound like the thin flutter of a cracked rib. Too early for another treatment. Too late to think what could have been different today to let sleep come tonight. Again. Breathe slowly, softly on the exhale. One, two, three, four. Lengthen the count of the exhale. Try to make it to three. Try to make it to four. Don't inhale too deeply and start the coughing. Cement nostrils, concrete sinus cavities. Last week had been different.

Last week she'd smelled seven times. The first, lemon scented soap she was packaging for a visit two hundred miles south where old friends waited, had lifted the top off her head to let the soft breeze of it right in. As good as the day Gail came all the way across town to make Grandmother's chicken soup. As wonderful as finding the all-night folk music program on Wednesdays. She smelled. She could smell! And, as always after some basic improvement, she wondered how she'd managed before. How long since she'd smelled? How many meals without aroma in a diet already tasteless by the confines of the diet? Thirty days? Sixty? Maybe since the beginning. One year, nine months. The congestion had come first so it made sense she'd lost her smell early on. An unappreciated sense. Its gradual disappearance unnoticed in the constant static of emotions; "What's happening to me?" "What should I do?" "Am I gonna die?" These enormous unanswerable questions, like childhood's "Does God love me?" "Does anyone feel what I feel?" Over time she'd stopped asking for God and gotten answers to some of the others. Not answers she'd expected. "What should I do?" "Try another cup of warm water?" "Eat a rice cake?" "How's the nausea tonight? Okay? Good." The dialogue going both ways now. "Does anyone feel what I feel?" Gail felt how she felt and Gail felt different. The fun was in separating it. Fun?

A half hour gone into the past now. The breath noise had grown no matter how carefully she manipulated her diaphragm. And she needed quick gasps now and then in the exhales to keep her panic down. The gut, the tickle, the cough, the asthma. Maybe she should try the machine again. Tonight was not being good. Tonight might become a time like before, cause her to wonder if these simple answers improved or pacified her. Tonight might be a night when all questions and answers were tricks of self-hate to take her attention from where it was needed. Maybe she should cry now and see if some of the tension would go. But crying would bring on the headache she'd get later from the drugs and play hell with the snot still damming her sinuses. Excuses. She was afraid to cry so early in the evening. Afraid to feel the despair and helplessness below the surface. Lynn said to know herself as getting better. Lynn said she saw her getting better; eyes clearer, sleep longer and deeper. Not tonight (shut up.) Lynn said these happy pictures might not heal you but you sure would stay sick without them. And she could trust Lynn (a little) because Lynn struggled too; allergies, sensitive skin, chronic acne, painful guts, vaginal infections, bronchitis, headaches, insomnia. Lynn knew any answers were like planting the smallest seedlings in an acre of garden. A gasp. Try to remember now. Where had the needles and amps of epinephrine ended up in the cleaning? Two months since she'd given herself a shot. Could she do it? Sure.

Hardly anyone died in North America of asthma any more. Almond had looked it up. "Asthma is rarely fatal." And "Diarrhea is the most common cause of death in the world." Questions and questions but what was her basic belief? Lynn said believe she would be well, was well in the center force of herself. Yes. She was well, was strong and vibrant. And sometimes strong vibrant healthy women lived in dying bodies. (Shut up!) This is only a question to pretend such questions matter. What matters is breathing carefully and slowly. The pee bucket was filling. Good. Already some water had worked its way through. Amazing body.

Four A.M. Twilla knocked. "How're you doing?" Her room nested at this end of the hall. "Do you want a shot?"

Hours and hours. It had been so long and she'd done so well. Tonight she'd stay out of the hospital. "How are you doing?" She could barely talk, her voice a whisper. A careful, careful whisper. An hour ago she'd been gasping, eyes bulging, bladder control lost, peeing on the bed and everywhere. An hour ago she thought she would die, had waited too long to call someone and now would stop breathing with everyone in the house peacefully asleep. Searing pain at the end of each breath, that endless end before she could open her mouth and try once more to force air inside. An hour ago she looked like the TV show where the hero's girlfriend dies with a knife in her back and it's a convincing death scene. She knew she looked that way. Twilla had seen her death gasps before. So had five or six others. Shawn said she was a private person, but Shawn had seen this. Then, somewhere between an hour ago and now, she had begun to drop off between pains. She still pounded her fist into her thigh to feel something other than that pain; but more and more, between the coughing aches her fingers were loose on the blanket.

"I was going to wait fifteen more minutes and then do a shot," she said.

"Here, let me," Twilla said. "You've been coughing for a long time. Where's your alcohol?"

Angel sagged and lost control of the exhale. Talking interrupted her concentration, a current of breathlessness pierced her from heart to butt. Her spine shot acid to her knee. Would she throw up? Stop breathing? Something. Please. She inhaled, heard Twilla.

"Just a little pinch. here we go." Twilla threw the little baseball toward her bone, the needle quick, cool alcohol swab. Breathe. One, two, three, four. Soon she could be at four for a second and relax. The synthetic adrenalin would last fifteen minutes. If she'd figured right, if her calm was right, that might do it for tonight. If not, if the pain and gasping returned she could do another shot. Two shots and she'd get a drug headache; three shots and they have to go to the hospital, argue with doctors not to put her on steroids. Better to breathe now. Better to wait, stay in control until the shot could be an extra boost at the end. She didn't want to go to the hospital.

"How're you doing now?" Twilla's arm squeezed tight on her shoulder. (I'm here. I care.)

She answered at the end of another ragged rip of fear; anus, spine, lightening, "50-50. Thank you." Pulled the hand from her shoulder and covered it with her own. "Thank you."

"Maybe you should try some codeine," Twilla said.

One, two, three, four. Think of something. Those seven smells. The peppermint soap, no, the lemon soap. The enchilada sauce. The stinking tar from a roadside factory right before we hit the San Onofre nuclear plant. Radiation doesn't smell. Almond said that was the worst part of the trip for her, finding the twin domed plant instead of the beach. Breathe. One, two, three. Seven smells. Enchilada sauce, factory stink, the seaweed smell of the San Diego beach. Almond hadn't noticed until she'd said. That sudden memory of David and herself come down here to swim naked and fall exhausted in the sand. David never believed in towels. "Dry with the sun," he said. She'd taken her body for granted. Oh, it wasn't so strong maybe but was getting there, with exercise it would be steadily stronger, so predictable. How to describe that smell? One, two, three, four. Wish she could go back and smell it again. Tangy. Salt tang. She thought it was rot the first time she'd smelled it. Now it was so good to smell, rot or not. The stale urine in the pee pitcher. Embarrassing. How long had it been sitting in her room getting gross and no one said anything. She should know a quick morning rinse wasn't enough. Plastic holds smells. She used being sick to get lazy. (NO!) She would rinse it more often, that's all. What else? The magnolia at the park, the armpits of a shirt. That's six. No, seven. There must have been eight then, because there was the peanut butter. Almost handing it back. "Can you smell this? No? Try to hold it closer." Yes. Yes, I can smell.

That was the peanut butter that went rancid and she didn't know. Had gas pains for days and no one thought to check her food. She didn't, couldn't have normal problems. All her problems had to be this overwhelming sickness. Pretty funny. She still didn't know how much of the gut pain was left over from the peanut butter. Twilla curled on the end of the bed sleeping.

"Codeine. Codeine," she'd said. Twilla doing so good for her but sometimes getting up in the middle of the night is hard for her. She wants me to get better. I want me to get better. But she offers easy solutions these nights sometimes. Codeine, steroids. "Come on. Take the drugs and be good. Let me sleep." She doesn't deal with the depression that comes after two nights of codeine. The steroids as powerful as any LSD and a list of side effects long as this night. That doctor yesterday. "Don't ask so many questions." "It's very predictable for this time of the year." "Allergy season." The doctor she'd come to trust after going through so many, her subtle maneuvers among the residents of the welfare hospital to find this one who listened. Even this one got tired and busy. Try this set of drugs and here's something for your nose. Predictable season. If it was so predictable, why didn't he warn her? Damn him. Damn them all. I will get well and I'll do it the best I know how. So what, I'm peeing on myself in buses? So what I beg twenty dollars from friends to try the vitamins? I will get better or I won't get better but I'm not gonna give my body to anyone except when and where I choose. I haven't come this far to die cursing someone for not taking care of me right. I'll decide how and when I'll feel this pain. That's what it comes down to anyway. One, two, three, four. Four.

Better. I could try putting my head a little lower. Where's that pile of pillows? The synthetic one Lynn gave me to trade for my feathers. Twilla's pretty gray-blue nylon case over it. Three pillows and I can almost lie on them and still breathe. Doing better. Definitely better. Gotta find the little one with Grandmother's embroidery to put under my side.

"Twilla, honey. You can go back to bed now if you want."

"You sure?"

"90-10. I think we've got it now."

"You're getting to be an expert."

"Who else?" Laughter. Sleep.

Shit: worms, yellow-brown. *Asthma:* slight wheeze. *Guts:* some tenderness and pain, allowable. *Tongue:* raw. *Nose:* congested, occasionally air through one nostril. *Emotions:* release, euphoria, lonely, tired. *Mind:* strong, clear, tired. *Time:* 5 A.M.

Leslie A. Donovan

For a Paralyzed Woman Raped
and Murdered While Alone
in Her Own Apartment

Nights like these
strangeness crouches at the edge of shadows,
even the TV sounds foreign, cold, inhuman—
but there is nothing
though every creak finds my body frightened,
hopeless as the primeval rattle sounding
beneath a rock just stepped on—
I see her alone in that apartment
Chaucer open before her, a desk lamp craning
above the page, its light glinting
off her wheelchair and
I tell myself it's a silly woman these days who
imagines in the dark like a helpless child,
overwhelmed by being alone
still every moment each unshuttered window seems
to beckon forward a dense shape
faceless, full of force—
the neighbors didn't hear her deadbolt
rip clear of the door and the
house is framed in suppressed terror—
the curve of my antique rocker is suddenly
a threat stretched just beyond the corner of my eye
I search my rooms for brass candlesticks
and aerosol cans
considering how ash trays and
hardbound books might be used as weapons—
Chaucer might have helped her if she
had been able to lift it above his thigh.

My collie finds me
by the phone forbidding myself to cry over a busy signal
he leans against me, pretending I am an oak tree
though we both know better
my fingers lose themselves blessedly in his fur

thinking how simple—sweet the relief
of his known body near me
its thickness allows my tears and
his bulk, warm and supportive
as Alexander's Great Horse becomes a shield
acknowledging the vulnerability I would deny
while the terrible strangeness of that other's body
stays with her forever in the helplessness of such nights
and I stay in the dark by the phone
gripping great tufts of fur
as if to hold him between me and
the strangeness of this night, her memories.

Barbara Ruth ————————————————————————

In My Disabled Women's Group

In my disabled women's group
The facilitator asked me
"What goals do you have
For yourself in the next five months?"
I felt the panic rise in me
Thinking of the days
Without a job
The weeks without the money
Or the energy
To move my furniture
From the garage where it is stored
Six hundred miles away.
How many times will my stomach hurt
In the next five months?
How many times will I throw up?
How many times will I go to the welfare office?
In the last three weeks
I've been seven times, and still no check.
I remember articles I've read on time management.
How you plot out goals
For the next ten years

Then one year
Then six months
One month
This week
Then you figure out
What you're going to do that day
And how it relates to the master plan.
I realize her question is quite reasonable
It's what other people do.
I don't live that way, anymore
I divide the days into smaller sections—
A whole day is too much pain
Too much responsibility to get through.
It started in the hospital
When I got morphine every three hours.
I'd watch the clock: the shot took 45 minutes to take effect
Then I slept for an hour and a half
Then 45 minutes till I could have another.
It's the way I passed the days.
Now, I divide it up with vitamins
I tell myself if I'm still awake at midnight
I'll take another C; calcium if I haven't got to sleep by 1:00.
I write down the things I have to do
On a good day I'll have checked off almost half the list.
Five months from now? Maybe if I'm lucky
I'll be living then
A whole day at a time.

Barbara Ruth · 33

Dale Brown

Learning to Work

MY FIRST JOB

My first day of my senior year in high school, I eagerly applied for jobs. A drugstore manager hired me as a waitress. I was very excited. Two dollars and sixty-five cents an hour seemed like a fortune to me. And I was thrilled to have my first job. I did not know at that time that I was "learning disabled."

My first impression was of noise and brightness. Cash registers clattered. Dishes crashed. Silverware clanged. We picked up our large white aprons from a hook next to a steel steaming sink. To one side of a narrow aisle was a shiny counter where the customers ate. On the other side was the grill, the bins of food, the soda machines, and the silverware and dishes.

Pam, a slender, young woman explained the system. "First, you take the order." She handed me a green pad. "Put it in your pocket. We're each assigned a section. You can help me with my section today, because it's a training day. Anyway, my section is here." She gestured, but I didn't know where she was pointing. "OK, just watch me." She approached a customer and said, "May I take your order please?" The customer told her and she wrote it down. I leaned over her shoulder to watch but she pushed me gently away. I didn't see what she did.

"One hamburger," she shouted to the cook.

"Now we have to make the tuna salad. Here's the scoop. You put the lettuce on the plate like this, then put the tuna on top. Then you put the tomato here."

Pam and I had to lean close to the counter to avoid being hit by a man carrying trays and the other passing people. I tried to watch her as she put the order together, but could barely follow.

"Show me how to do the tuna salad again?" I asked. "I don't remember how to do it."

"I can't until we get another order for it. Now, we clean up the counters by putting the dishes down here. Roy takes them later . . ."

She spent the day talking to me and telling me detail after detail. I tried to listen to her, but the other conversations, the sizzling of the grill, and the rushing of water distracted me.

"How do you take an order again?" I asked.

"It's easy," she replied. "All you have to do is to write down what they say and then get the prices."

The next day, my own section was assigned to me. Fortunately, my shift began at 2 P.M., which was "off hours" and there were only two customers. A man and a woman were waiting expectantly. The man asked for a hamburger and coke. The woman asked for a tuna salad and root-beer. I wrote down the order, but didn't know the prices.

"How much is a hamburger?" I asked Pam.

"Eighty-five cents."

"How about a Coke?"

"Was it large or small?"

"I didn't ask."

"Better find out."

"How much is a tuna salad?"

"45¢. Look at the menu, next time. It has all of the prices."

I went to make the tuna salad. I couldn't find the scoop and had to ask Pam for it. The plates had disappeared. Again, I had to interrupt her. I laid down the lettuce, but it wouldn't lie flat. Then I couldn't scoop the tuna. I tugged into it with the rounded scoop, but didn't know how to press the handle to let the tuna out in a ball. So I ended up spooning it on the lettuce and hoping it was enough. Then I gave the woman her tuna salad.

I checked my list and brought their drinks, using the first paper cups my hand encountered. I couldn't easily see the difference between large and small, and by now I had forgotten Pam's reminder.

"Where's my hamburger?" asked the man.

"Oh, I'm sorry, I forgot to tell the cook," I replied. "One hamburger," I shouted to him. Fortunately, there was already a hamburger next to him, so I took it and gave it to my customer. I was feeling quite proud of myself for serving my first order and relaxed for a moment.

"Listen, don't steal my hamburger again," said Pam.

"What do you mean?"

"You know what I mean! The cook made that hamburger for my customer, your's is just now being made! Don't do that again!"

I approached two other customers to take their order. They both ordered hotdogs and tea.

"Where's our check?" asked the first man I had served.

I gave him the check. He looked at it thoughtfully, "How much are we supposed to pay?" he asked.

"I don't know," I said and took the check back. Panic hit. How much were the cokes? I made up a price of 30¢, then concentrated on adding them up.

"You owe us $1.90," I told him, handing him the check back.

"Where are our hotdogs?" asked one of my customers.

"And my order?" said another person.

I ignored them.

"You overcharged us for the cokes," said the man. "They cost 25¢."

"O.K.," I said.

"We owe you $1.80," he said.

I approached the huge-looking cash register. I had forgotten how to work it.

"Pam, you need to show me how to work the cash register."

"I showed you that yesterday."

"Sorry, you need to show me again."

She rang up my order, without telling me what she was doing. When the numbers $1.90 came up, I said, "I'm sorry. I made a mistake. I overcharged them for the Cokes. They're 25¢, but I didn't change it on my order form."

She glared at me. "Now we have to make a void slip." She turned on a small microphone. "Mr. Connors, please come to the counter. Mr. Connors, to the counter."

I waited. "Dale, don't you have any other orders to take?" she asked.

I nodded. I had lost the order slip. I checked my pad, my pockets, the floor around me, I would have to ask them again. But who were they? I couldn't remember their faces!

"Dale, come here," said Pam. Mr. Connors was working at the cash register.

He looked at me sympathetically.

"You'll catch on soon," he said. "It's only your second day." He showed me how to use the cash register and said, "Try not to make too many voids."

I reached into my pocket and fortunately, the order slip was there.

"Dale, your customers are building up. I'm going to take care of those two and you finish your order," said Pam.

How did she do it, I wondered. She moved efficiently and effortlessly, taking orders, preparing food, and ringing things up.

I brought the hotdogs to the next customers.

The first few days were a blur of confusion and errors. Other employees were kind to me at first, but rapidly grew impatient as I constantly asked questions. I couldn't memorize the prices, despite studying the menu during breaks and even taking one home to work on it. I kept on forgetting where the plates, silverware, and tools were located.

"Where's the scoop?" I asked Pam once.

"Right in front of your nose," she replied. She pointed to it, and suddenly it appeared. Today, I know that this is a typical symptom of visual figure-ground problems, but at that time I didn't understand why things disappeared and then, suddenly, reappeared.

Preparing food was difficult, even after learning how to do it. For example, to fix a coke, one took a paper cup and pushed it against a knob under the nozzle. It required a lot of seltzer water and a small amount of coke syrup. I couldn't tell the difference between the knob for seltzer water and the knob for coke syrup. The left knob and the right knob seemed the same and so did the two labels. My only choice was to squirt a little bit of liquid into the cup, check and see which it was. Then if it was coke syrup, I had to remember to only put a little bit of it and a lot of seltzer water. Since the coke syrup looked like a coke, it was easy to serve a lot of syrup with a tiny bit of seltzer water. The customers would comment on my funny tasting cokes!

I never figured out the sequence of putting an order together. Now, it seems clear that you start with the cooked items and work on your other food while they are cooking. With my inability to conceive of time properly, it was not obvious, and nobody told me. So I always served my customers their food at different times.

I had trouble walking back and forth in the small space between the counter and food preparation area. I often bumped into other workers or dropped things. Once, I dropped and broke a tray of glasses.

Because of difficulty in seeing and remembering faces clearly, I often confused customers' orders. I concentrated hard on each face. Sometimes I would count and write the number of stools from one end. Unfortunately, I often miscounted or skipped one of the stools. Once, I wrote down "blonde hair and blue eyes." The customer laughed when she saw that. A few times, I went down the aisle and said, "Who ordered the hamburger and coke?" Someone always took them.

Gradually, I mastered the cash register, although I had a tendency to punch the wrong numbers and end up with $13.80 instead of $1.38. The tax table print was so small that I sometimes guessed the tax or forgot it all together.

My favorite job was going to the stockroom to get ice. The other waitresses hated it. I loved it and got almost all of the ice. I would walk downstairs holding two buckets, one in each hand. Then, I'd sit on a carton for a few minutes to calm myself. Then I'd fill each bucket with a scoop, enjoying the rhythm of the ice hitting the bucket. When they were full, I took them upstairs and poured one into each icebin.

I was cheerful and most of my customers were sympathetic. Whenever they pointed out my errors, I apologized and immediately corrected them before going on to my next orders. I asked them to find the prices on the menu. I'd often ask, "Have I forgotten anything? Can I do something else?"

Due to my cheerfulness, reliability about coming in on time, and obvious eagerness to please, the manager liked me. Sometimes, Mr. Conners kidded me about all of my void slips, but he was very patient. My coworkers, on the other hand, had to constantly answer my questions and correct my errors. Even though I took care of some of the unpopular jobs, they found me difficult and were undoubtedly glad when I had to leave, due to a change in bus schedule.

Later, I had many jobs. I was a salesperson in a department store during Christmas rush. You can imagine the problems! At Pitzer College, I woke up at 6 A.M. to clean the dormitory kitchens. I loved that job, because I worked alone and at my own pace. After transferring to Antioch College, I became a cafeteria worker and served food, washed dishes, and helped the cooks. I did each job better than the last.

DISCOVERING MY LEARNING DISABILITIES

As I worked, I often wondered why I had to try so hard. Everyone else could do the work so easily. They picked it up quickly, not needing as much training and attention from the supervisor. If I concentrated hard and did everything correctly, I was accused of being too slow. On the other hand, when I went faster, I made errors. Other people could do the job correctly and at the right speed. No one else had to work during the breaks or worse, punch out then return to complete undone tasks.

The answer to that question came after working at an electronics factory during a work-study quarter. There, I realized that I must have some kind of specific problem. My productivity was very low. For example, we had to strip wires, cutting one layer of wires with a razor blade, without cutting into the next layer of plastic. I had trouble using the right amount of pressure. Either, I'd cut into the next layer of wires or not cut through the first layer. Sometimes the thin copper wires broke as I twisted them. I often cut my fingers.

One day my supervisor asked me to strip "eighty" wires. I was doing the job, when she said, "Dale, it's taking you an awfully long time to strip those eight wires."

"You said eighty wires," I replied, surprised.

"I said eight."

"No, you said eighty."

"I said eight!"

"I heard eighty," I replied. What was it? Was it my hearing? It had been tested several times and was considered good. Yet, there was no question that I often misheard instructions. I knew about my clumsiness and difficulty in seeing correctly. But I had assumed my hearing was fine.

After leaving that job, I visited a counselor who told me that my mistakes were similar to those of children with something called learning disabilities. She sent me to the library to read about the topic. At that time, learning disabilities were assumed to be outgrown in early adulthood. My research was revealing. My handicap had a name! There was a reason for all that extra hard work! Each problem was actually a symptom of a disability. If only someone had recognized all of that extra effort. For a few weeks I felt sorry for myself and wished for the praise that was deserved, but never received.

Basically, however, information about my learning disability was very useful. Weaknesses, I realized, could be worked on systematically. For example, many learning disabled people can't use one side of the body well. In my case, I dropped things because the muscles of my right arm would suddenly relax. So I decided to carry items with the weight on my left arm. That solved that problem.

My knowledge of my learning disabilities was particularly essential during my first job after college graduation, working as a court reporter. Obviously, this was not the right job for me. However, during the recession of 1975, there were very few jobs, and I was lucky to get one, even as a court reporter. I had been searching for five months when I applied for the job. Helen, who directed the company, showed me a large black box, which stood as high as my hip.

"Can you lift that?" she asked.

I picked it up, keeping a straight face and hiding my breathlessness.

She nodded. "There will be two of these and you will have to carry them all over the place." She told me that I would be responsible for taping the trials so that the typist could produce an accurate transcript.

Listening to her, I wondered if I could do the job. Clearly, I'd go right up against my learning disabilities. With inaccurate hearing, vision, and touch, it would be a challenge to do the job correctly. But I needed a job! So I enthusiastically sold myself during the interview. They chose me.

On my first work day, they assigned Paul to show me how to use the equipment. Now that I could realize that it was impossible for me to learn it all the first time, I relaxed and absorbed as much as possible. . . .

When Paul took me to a trial where he was recording, I watched carefully and asked questions. At the end of the day, I still did not understand what to do, although the major points were becoming clear.

"I'm sorry, but I still don't feel ready to work on my own," I said. "Can I spend tomorrow watching another reporter?" He asked Helen, who let me have several extra training days.

Our training paid off. While it took me longer to record trials, the transcribers told my boss that they liked to receive my work because it was easy to follow. And, once, a judge requested me.

MEETING OTHER LEARNING DISABLED PEOPLE

But my hunt for a more appropriate job continued. Finally, a professional association hired me as an office manager. This job also required overcompensation. My work week was about sixty hours long. The business manager jokingly threatened to charge me rent because I was there so often.

During this job, I often felt lonely. I had finally found a professional job in which I could succeed and advance. But the price was spending most of my time in the office. Was life only work? I decided to seek out other people with disabilities. Since the handicap is invisible, forming a self-help group seemed the only way to meet others. Thus, I started the Association of Learning Disabled Adults (ALDA). Meeting other learning disabled people made me realize how severe our handicaps are. Many people in ALDA couldn't even hold a job. Either they couldn't find one or they were frequently fired.

We had no access to help from professionals, since we supposedly outgrew our disabilities. Our problems were considered minimal. We were told that we weren't trying or that we were being careless. The help we could give each other was our only chance. But that should not have been. We deserved the help that people with visible handicaps received.

I decided to look for work in an organization that dealt with disabled people. There, I could learn about the field and tell other people about learning disabilities. . . . One group that interested me was the President's Committee on Employment of the Handicapped. I visited them and read a tall stack of publications from their stockroom. One was by Bob Ruffner, their Director of Communications. I wrote to him and complimented him on his article. He responded by arranging to meet me and have me interviewed by the Committee's magazine, *Disabled USA*. . . .

A job opened up at the Committee. I filled out form after form, and after five months of being interviewed, of waiting, or refilling forms, of competing against many other qualified men and women, I got the job! Today, I am on the Committee staff, promoting opportunities for disabled people through writing, public speaking, and special events. I enjoy the work, doing things that I'm good at. My job can be done in a reasonable amount of time.

It has not been easy for me to find my place in society as an LD adult. It took hard work, self-discipline, and positive thinking. I had to demand the training that was needed in each situation. . . .

On the other hand, I was born with many advantages. My family was warm and supportive. They paid for my college education. It was always clear to me that blue-collar work was temporary. What happens to people with these disabilities who are raised in factory towns? Or those who cannot afford a college degree? Or those who are not intelligent or emotionally stable? What happens if you are not qualified to be a professional, but can't do entry-level jobs either? These are the people we must help. I hope my story gives some clues as to how.

Seal-Woman

Seal-Woman   your world is Antarctica.
Your flippers flopped you unto land
barren but for the accumulation of ice.
You drag half your weight like a sack
of wet sand behind you.
You bark, but your barks hang hollow
like announcements of your name
into a vacant place,
follow your shallow trench track
like young.

Seal-Woman   your skin
isn't like department store coats, your fur
is dull, is matted, is thin.
You move as though you had no destination.
Are you hunting? Aren't you hungry?

Consider the cycles:
A thaw could find you
in water, you could glide
like the rhythm of music,
you could be graceful with those flippers,
with that enormous heavy tail.
Your skin would thicken, your coat glisten;
Fish would surround you in schools.

Land-Woman   how hard it is
for you to be a seal.
Dive. Dive down where seaweed
and coral are living flowers,
where sand is cast off as pearls,
where flying fish and porpoises leap
into the weightlessness of air.

Leslie A. Donovan

Self-Portrait

Sun-scoured
sharpened white as bone
taut as the muscles of lovers
her limbs
ask timid questions of the sky
voiceless branches
mazes resolved in yearnings
seek ways to intersect
the winged others
but find stillness
her only option.

Twigs hunger
for another span upward
another length to entice
the sparrow's choice
the acknowledgment from above
through contact between bird and branch
Yet past storms and too early springs
ring by ring
have bent her direction
solid and uncorrectable
the sun's distance verifies it
fused in place
as fossils into stone.

Her nature
forbids motion though
stillness is such a painful effort
and she craves
movement's honesty when
leafing so green
she is almost golden
she yields up
what sleeps fallow and deep
within
but the robins
nest elsewhere.

Lame

Several words describe the person who cannot walk in an ordinary fashion. My own personal preference is "physically limited" for a rather formal description and plain, old-fashioned "lame" as a short (and somehow *loving*) adjective. "Orthopedically handicapped" is fair enough. But here I conjure up visions of huge rehabilitation clinics or state senators reading amendments in proper medical and legal terms. The two words together are exact but cold. "Handicapped" alone is far too inclusive to apply with much realism to those who cannot walk well, for it has become a grab-bag word that embraces an enormous population of deaf, blind, speech-impaired, and mentally impaired individuals.

"Disabled" goes "handicapped" one better. Here there are legal overtones. To be classified as "disabled" one usually needs a medical stamp to prove inability to earn a living, and this can apply to anyone who is out of commission from a physical or mental illness. Yet both "handicapped" and "disabled" are handy tags to hang on those who get around with crutches or a walker or a wheelchair. They slip out in ordinary conversation and who am I to mind? I use the words myself.

But "crippled" is an ugly and stumbling word. There is no dignity there at all—only a picture of someone twisted, pitiful, poor, and not very bright. This is a personal prejudice that took hold long ago for reasons sunk deep in the subconscious. But I find when I use "crippled," I am stressing the harshness and purely *physical* fact of paralysis. The word, in its dark intensity, blots out the power and the hope of the spirit.

Of course, "lame" is not an accurate description for a person who cannot walk at all; only paralyzed applies here. But, oh, the hope for improvement embodied in the word "lame"! Perhaps that is one of its appealing connotations, suggesting a mild affliction, though sometimes a stretching of the truth. Once I received a letter from a friend who had a slow recovery from a fall, and she mentioned with beautiful carelessness that we had so much in common with our children and "our lameness." I treasure her conception of me not as disabled or crippled or even handicapped, but simply lame. She is right. To be able to walk with crutches, even though one must resort to a wheelchair in some situations, should classify a person as "lame" if she wishes.

I should like to resurrect the word "lame" because it is gentle and informal. Though there is often more to it than that, we who walk with difficulty are primarily lame and far more fortunate than those thousands of men, women, and children who cannot leave their wheelchairs at all. If "lame" should seem a vague term like "thin" or "fat" or "pretty," so much the better. Most of us would like nothing more than to melt in with the crowd—unlabeled, almost unnoticed.

We had a cat once who appeared, half-starved, at the door to request family membership along with three other cats. One of her paws took a very long time to reach the ground, so she devised an alternate way to walk, scorning the slow limp, and she simply hopped like a rabbit with her three strong legs. Still she had to rest a lot. Fortunately for her, cats have few responsibilities beyond self-preservation and cleanliness and she could accomplish those near the house. The other cats were quite gentle with her, as if they sensed she couldn't handle a hard fight. Yet she was expected to make her own way. No one put a supper dish under her nose or pushed her onto safe high ground in the midst of a dog attack.

And so it was for many of us who went home from a long hospitalization [for polio] thirty years ago. There was no real follow-up care as there is now. We were on our own, especially if we lived far from therapists and the orthopedic specialists who were working full time on new polio cases anyway.

It became a very personal matter between you and your stubborn body. Certain maneuvers failed, and so you tried others. There was a bit of black magic to these first attempts because you didn't plan consciously to get up from a chair in a specific way that came as an inspiration in the middle of the night. Rather you were propelled by a mysterious force—the driving power of muscles unknown to you—to move your body this way or that until something worked. Babies know this. Their first tentative steps are individual tries at speeding life up a bit. They see people *walking*—a truly fascinating activity. No one lectures them with the scientific approach of a quadracep muscle straining to pull in a forward motion. First one little leg, then another; try and fail; try and fail. If babies stopped to analyze or criticize each attempt, the discouragement level would be too much. Instead their innocent minds shed worry and gather faith that nature has a formula for walking—never mind what it might be.

During my first few weeks at home I discovered from nowhere that I could lock my leg braces, turn around in a chair, stiffen my arms, push with the strong left bicep muscle, and back off to a standing position. This opened up a whole new world. I could grab my crutches and practice walking any old time. Alone. Nature (that old black magic) was on my side. Together we backed into a way of life with the premise that any attempt at motion was better than none at all. Even with an incorrect gait, frightening falls, and the speed of a tortoise, the upright approach beat years in a wheelchair.

My ingenious husband designed stools, ramps, arm slings, and kitchen equipment so that we could remain an independent family. Having been separated too long by war and a wayward virus, we wanted to take care of each other again. There was a strong natural incentive to adjust. But, for my part, I did a most imperfect job. I was asked many times during the first year at home, and am still asked, "How in the world do you manage?" The answer remains, "Not very well. Just average." Sometimes an abundance of love rather than determination makes things possible, if not smooth-running.

Vassar Miller

Insomniac's Prayer

I lie with my body knotted into a fist
clenching against itself,
arms doubled against my ribs
knees crooking into a gnarl,
legs, side by side, martialed.

My sleep is a war against waking up,
my waking up is a slow raveling again into dark
when dreams jump out of my skull
like pictures in a child's pop-up book
onto paper if my luck can catch them
before they dribble away into dingy dawns.

Oh, who will unsnarl my body
into gestures of love?
Who will give my heart room
to fly free in its rickety cage?
Whose subtlety whisper apart my legs,
thrusting quick like a snake's tongue?
Who will nudge the dreams back into my head,
back into my bones, where rhyming with one another
like wind chimes,
they will make music whenever I move?

Part II
Seeking Help and Love

Disability is more than a physical condition. It can potentially affect all aspects of our being in the world but has a special significance in our interpersonal relationships. Our disability may affect our family members, lovers or spouses, coworkers, friends. The stories, poems, and essays in Part 2 explore the impact of other people's feelings about our disabilities, as well as how our disabilities affect the way we feel about and behave toward others.

These works roughly follow the chronology of a woman's life, describing childhood relationships with parents, grandparents, and caretakers, then relationships with peers and friends in adolescence and early adulthood, and concluding with works about adult relationships and parenthood, including reflections on growing older and on facing death.

Our relationships with our parents or early parental figures shape our lives more than any others. For those of us who are born with a disability or acquire one in childhood, how our parents regard us and our disability largely determines our sense of self-worth and our ability to function independently and interdependently in adulthood. In "On Oxfords and Plaster Casts," Roberta Cepko celebrates her mother's determination to let her grow up with minimal stigma attached to her surgeries and physical differences. In the poem "Bedtime Story," Murielle Minard tells of her mother's stalwart hope for cure. Mary Grimley Mason's "The Bargain" shows a child's devotion to and identity with her grandmother, and her perception of God's power over death and disability. In "Living Upstairs, Leaving Home, and at the Moscow Circus," Cheryl Davis describes her struggles to gain recognition of her real needs as a disabled person in her family and then her quest for and success in achieving interdependence Nancy Mairs offers an elegiac reflection on the death of her father in the poem "Conversations at All Hours."

The conflict between the needs to achieve independence and to acknowledge dependence on others can be especially severe for disabled women. Perhaps stemming from our frontier history, ours is a culture of "do it yourselfers." There are very few of us able, as the popular psychological theories espouse, to "ask for what we need." The disabled person who requires substantial help in managing her day-to-day life is often confused and angered by her dependency. On the other hand, disabled people are commonly badgered by well-meaning and sometimes humorous would-be assistants who "help" the blind woman across the street against her will, or rush to open the door for a mobility-impaired person, thereby impeding her exit. This confusion about help is one of the more devastating aspects of the experience of disability, and can be far more painful than the physical problems and treatments. Examples of this conflict and confusion are particularly apparent in the health-care setting. While almost every health-care worker is motivated by human caring, the structure of the system often interferes with the patient's receipt of the kind of respectful and humane treatment that would foster independence, assertiveness, and positive identity. The role of patient is a powerless one, especially for the female patient in the male-dominated medical world. Marsha Saxton, in her essay, "The Something That Happened before I Was Born," reveals the impact of her repeated hospitalizations as a child.

We are women. We share with all women the needs for love, companionship, and sexual intimacy. Disabled women may have loving relationships with men or women, in the manner of all women. In the realm of sexuality, disabled women are denied acceptance because of the stereotype that equates disability with asexuality. Black women also speak of feeling asexualized by the culture in relation to the dominant group of white women. Perhaps it is in the nature of being devalued that we women of difference are not regarded as truly female. Other myths affecting the perception of disability and sexuality include the idea that disability may be contagious and that sex is somehow a rare commodity that should be reserved for highly-valued people, that is, the attractive and able-bodied.

Many of the selections in this part speak of the difficulty of getting beyond these myths and stereotypes, of the striving toward connection and intimacy. They reveal both the pain of deprivation and the strength to be found in the closeness and support of friends and lovers. Debra Kent's essay, "In Search of Liberation," outlines the need for new sexual role models for disabled women. Leslie A. Donovan's poem, "Recurrences," illustrates the same point, declaring, "In my back, a metal rod won't let me bend like Scarlett O'Hara into your arms." Jean Stewart's poem, "Incidental," suggests that the presence of disability, because of the need for physical assistance, may actually allow intimacy more easily. In "Recovery Poem #4," Barbara Ruth tells of the power of touch and tenderness.

Among the most sensitive issues facing disabled women are their right and ability to bear and rear children. Fears about the procreation of disabled people and other minorities led to the eugenics movement in the early 1900s. By 1937, 28 states had adopted eugenic sterilization laws aimed at persons with epilepsy, mental retardation, and other kinds of disabilities where procreation was deemed "unadvisable." Recent developments in genetic and reproductive technologies have contributed to a widespread trend to abort fetuses prenatally identified as disabled. This trend is largely based on erroneous ideas about the quality of life attainable by disabled people and assumes their lives are not worth living. Similarly, disabled mothers are often assumed to be incompetent and are denied custody of their children for this reason. Although disability does affect parenthood, frequently these difficulties can be overcome with planning and assistance. In her interview, "I'm on a Lot of Committees," Frances Deloatch shares her sorrow at being unable to have children, and her quest to find alternatives that allow her to be with them. In "Shape," Nancy Mairs explores the complex struggles of a mother with multiple sclerosis, who strives to cope with her adolescent children in the shadow of her divorce.

Other works in this section show how difficult it can sometimes be to get beyond the stereotypes. The speaker in Deborah Kendrick's poem, "For Tess Gallagher," shares her longing for connection and then her disappointment in failing to challenge the common patterns of interaction with a blind person. In the worst of times, intimacy and connection are our salvation, but breaking through the isolation is not a simple matter of "reaching out"; the barriers are great. In the poem "By Her Hands," Rebecca Gordon shows how disability affects a relationship that has been strong enough to survive it. The main character in "Significant Others" by Miriam Ylvisaker is embittered by her loneliness and her unfulfilled fantasies of love. The poem "I Met Florence in Room 43" by Kay Yasutome explores the deep need for a relationship with a disabled peer. Vassar Miller in "Faux Pas" and Adrienne Rich in "A Woman Dead in Her Forties" tell of the deaths of close friends, of what was not said.

The Something That Happened before I Was Born

What affected me most as a disabled child, I think, was being in the hospital so much. For several months every two years or so, I would go in for more surgery on my legs. I remember the feeling of dread when the letter from Shriner's Hospital arrived to announce my scheduled intake. Shriner's Hospital for Crippled Children, a charity hospital funded by wealthy business people and the East-West Football Game ("Strong legs run so that weak legs may walk") accepted me as a patient, though my parent's income was on the borderline of their income limits. We never could have afforded my surgeries without help.

I recall sitting in the rocker, my mother crying. I felt as if a big hand were reaching into our family to pluck me out. My parents seemed powerless; there was nothing they could do to prevent my leaving.

I remember, too, how little attention was paid to the surgery happening to help my legs work better. At the time, especially when I was young, that just seemed like a ruse to obscure what I knew was really true: my body was defective and so I had to be punished.

The hospital seemed to me like an orphanage. The other children seemed so disconnected from wherever they came; like me, they had been plucked from their homes to come to this place, "my second home," as my father called it. I was there during the 1950s and early 1960s, but the decor was of the 1920s and 1930s. On the wall murals, girls in ruffled bonnets and pantaloons and boys in knickers rolled wooden hoops. Our metal beds and high-sided cribs, even the night tables, were from that same era. The big TV's, one in each twelve-bed ward, were the only evidence of my own time.

My memories of the days there are of waiting, waiting for the surgery to happen. I was sometimes there for a month before the surgery was scheduled to occur.

In my earliest stays, before age six, the hospital allowed no visiting at all. They told my parents that this policy prevented the spreading of germs, but even at my young age, I realized they simply wanted to minimize contact, to keep our ward world separate from the one we knew outside. The children would have cried and complained, felt lonely and afraid, if their parents had been able to come in and hold them. Such was the hospital mentality in those days of the early 1950s; it was still a time to keep children passive and silent.

The families of patients gathered on Sunday afternoons outside the windows of our rooms. Inside, we'd try to talk through the screened openings. I vividly remember peering down at my parents and my brother fifteen feet below. I would try to smile and reassure them I was fine. My mother looked like she was about to burst into tears, and my father, behind his stories of what had been happening at home, looked nervous. My brother almost always looked puzzled.

Years later, in college, I read an article about the profound impact of lengthy parent-child separation on the emotional health of young children. I felt a pang of envy for those children whose mothers now stay overnight in the hospital with them, and I wondered about the hidden damage to my psyche.

The hospital conducted a kind of school for us, run by retired teachers and volunteers. We were given readers and math books and sat behind desks modified for wheelchairs. Classes consisted only of our reading lessons and answering questions on what we read. There were no open group discussions like those I enjoyed in my school at home. I always felt way behind at my school when I returned.

We also had crafts, which I enjoyed the most, partly because the volunteers in this class seemed more like the people I knew in my own world, and also because I loved the projects. We made lanyards, copper foil plaques, yarn dolls, and the like. In addition, I was given the privilege of using the sewing machine that belonged to the "Gray Ladies," a Red Cross volunteer group of older women who made the clothes we wore. (We weren't allowed to bring our own clothes or possessions.)

The Gray Ladies taught me how to knit and, while I waited for my surgery, I made many hats, scarfs, and vests. Then, during the longer time to heal and go home, I made more. It was only recently that I've been able to identify the feeling I get now, so many years later, when I pick up my knitting; it's a feeling of anxious waiting.

Sometimes the hospital had parties where clowns passed out ice cream and balloons and a man played the accordion or the piano. We sang, played bingo, and generally succeeded in making the room come alive. Then the party people would leave, and the wards seemed even emptier.

Unlike many of the children in the hospital, I could walk. As a result, during the waits for my surgery to be scheduled, I developed a game that was to set a life pattern for me. I would get things for others (comic books from the shelf) and fetch objects that had fallen from beds. I pretended I was a nurse, sometimes a doctor.

A patient in the hospital has a low status in our society; I opted for a higher one. I made myself a helper, someone with a purpose, a needed person. In my game, I created a reason for me to be. I was there to help the nurses clear the bed stands for the lunch trays, to fold the blankets, to fill the water glasses. I wandered around the ward and visited the other girls, the patients, asking them about themselves. "Did it hurt?" I'd ask. "Is there anything I can do?"

This game also took my mind off my loneliness, distracted me from my fear, and made me feel special. Soemtimes the aides let me come into the kitchen and preview the dinner menu. Or I was allowed to accompany a nurse on an errand to the administrative offices. The nurses liked me a lot, and when I would return a couple of years later, many immediately recalled my smile and sunny disposition.

I have a vivid memory of a nurse saying to me in earnest, "God made you pretty and sweet to make up for your being crippled." I listened to this and guessed it must be true, but still I puzzled at my images of some of the other children there, scarred from burns or drooling from cerebral palsy, who apparently hadn't received the same compensation. Why was I handicapped and still pretty? It seemed a contradiction to my child's mind.

The word *crippled* was ugly and repulsive. Could I be hiding my real self? What a remarkable deception! These thoughts sometimes haunted my childhood.

The scariest part of the hospitalization for me was not the surgery, but the doctor rounds. On the mornings when these rituals were scheduled, the nurses and aides awakened us much earlier than usual. Meals and wash-ups were rushed. Those of us who were up for discussion would be dressed in white canvas bikinis that exposed our bodies.

Then they would come, the surgeons, the residents, the interns. All men. On rare occasions a woman physical therapist accompanied them, but, like the nurses, she stood in back, out of the way, and never spoke unless she was asked for information.

They entered our ward, about fifteen adults, trailing a big X-ray viewing box with racks underneath for charts. One by one, we'd be discussed, some of us just briefly. Strange long words were uttered; bandages were opened and quickly closed. Our bones showed purple on the X-ray screen.

Others of us would be dealt with in detail, with great deliberation as to how our bodies could be changed and improved. I was often discussed in depth, such an interesting case, this spina bifida who could walk without braces, though slightly wobbily; whose bladder retained urine quite well, but needed to be catheterized; who was quite bright (no signs of hydrocephalus or subsequent retardation).

I was told to walk up and down the ward, naked in my white bikini, as the doctors watched and talked and pointed to the bones on the screen and the bones in my body. One would call me over to him and he'd flex my feet up and down, and command me to stand on my toes, to stand on one foot, to bend my knees. How hard I'd try to do it right, so maybe they'd leave my body the way it was. Maybe they wouldn't make me have surgery.

Once, a surgeon—the one who looked so stern—called me over and poked at my hips. I was alarmed; until now, this place on my body had always been left untouched. My hips, I thought, were okay as they were. The surgeon began to untie my bikini, and a flood of terror rushed through me. Would I be even more exposed to this crowd?

It was rare for me, the brave crippled child, to show or even to feel my fear. I had learned to retain my power by *not* expressing my rage or showing my tears. I wouldn't let them scold me or shame me for resisting their orders.

But now in this group, my fear took control and, shaking, I grasped at the cloth and stared up at the surgeon. Pleading-eyed, I begged him to let me keep this token of privacy. Miraculously, he let go. A nurse stepped over and wrapped a robe around me, closing the scene like a curtain. The surgeon and the rest moved on. I swallowed tears and marvelled at not being scolded.

My recollection of surgery is a dreamlike blur: being wheeled into the operating room, the green masked people speaking with no mouths. I tried to stay awake as long as I could, talking and asking furiously. I was never told beforehand what was going to happen to me; I was only given reassurances that I would be all right.

Hours later, I would awake. Fighting the numbness, I would peer down at my legs to see the white casts propped way up high on pillows. I'd recognize the toes peeking out of the bandages, pink from Merthiolate. Bottles of fluid, some red, some clear, hung over me, feeding tubes in my arms. I always woke up alone.

And always there was a stuffed animal placed in my bed, a gift from the hospital. I would stare at it, trying to be pleased at the dog or bear or rabbit, but also fighting the temptation to cry that was prompted by the safety of this new friend (who, unlike grown-up people, could really see what I was feeling).

And then I would call out for the nurse. A little later, she'd appear, almost invariably with needle in hand; she was assuming I'd choose the numbness over the pain and awareness. At this point, I would call into play one of the many tricks I'd developed to exert the small degree of child power I could: I would ask for food. Not because I wanted to eat, but because hunger, to the nurses, was a sure sign that I was okay. They wouldn't try to drug me again for now. They'd be impressed with my quick recovery, and I'd be praised as a good patient.

My tactic also assured that the nurse would have to return, possibly for as long as it took me to mouth the Jell-O. I'd eat it and struggle through the druggy fog to ask the nurse questions that would keep her with me. My mouth would be dry, my throat aching from the trache tube, my tongue sore from the clamp used to keep me from choking. And still I talked. I never cried or complained of pain; that would have driven her away.

In all my hospital experiences, the saddest part was always the same. All those people trying so hard to help me: the nurses, the doctors, the volunteers, the Shriners. All of them hoping for me to get better and do well, all wanting to be kind and useful, all feeling how important helping me was, yet never did any one of them ask me what it was like for me. They never asked me what I wanted for myself. They never asked me if I wanted their help.

The surgery I had was very successful. Doctors I see now still comment on the skilled work. But I do not feel entirely grateful. I feel, instead, a remote anger stored beneath my coping pattern of complacent understanding. People do the best they can to help in meaningful ways, I know. I just wish all disabled children would say to their helpers: "Before you do anything else, just listen to me."

Murielle Minard

Bedtime Story

Every night
My mother
Would massage my legs
With melted cocoa butter.
Up and down.
Slowly—
Faithful to the ritual,
She never spoke.
Only her strong hands
Insisting.

We both
Believed
It could undo
What had been done.

I do not remember
At what point
The ceremonies ended.

Roberta Cepko

On Oxfords and Plaster Casts

She had me at a time when the term was "crippled." "Handicap" was
then most frequently used in reference to golf competitions and wheelchairs were cumbersome clunks of steel and metal rarely seen outside of
hospital corridors and nursing homes. I fell into the life of Joan Stonic
Cepko one humid August morning—the last of her "gang," as she's often
called us—with my club feet and other disconcerting abnormalities that
might have sent a weaker person searching for an institution for the hope-
lessly afflicted. Or at least to a therapist for some expensive support. Or
perhaps today to a bottle of Valium.

My mother went home and sewed.

Maybe she even began the christening gown right there at the hospital—I wouldn't doubt it, for to this day she doesn't like her hands to be still. At any rate, she carefully tailored it to fit all nearly eight pounds of me and proceeded to embroider dainty curlicues and flowers all over the delicate cotton. Then she went out, bought a roll of film for her prized Brownie camera and blew the wad on her little oddball.

Was a time, mostly in my teens, when I yearned to probe her memory in depth about her reactions to my birth, to address her with questions like:

"Did you cry when you first saw me?"

"How did you feel when you first held my feet in the palms of your hands?"

"What were you thinking as the doctor spanked the breath into me?"

Was *anything* even said at first? I have wondered. There have always been, lurking in the back of my mind, many questions painful to contemplate yet burning to find utterance. But because I could never bear to see the hurt on Mom's face as I broached the subject, we have pushed it aside as a personal, perhaps inexpressible, moment in Mom's life that I will never enter into.

Besides, in some ways which I could never understand, Mom seemed to think my feet not repulsive, but actually *beautiful*. I recollect early evening baths when, in one of her soft terry towels, she cuddled those twisted feet—freed from plaster or braces. She gently rubbed them dry between the detergent-rough palms of her hands, almost as if my squat toes were made of porcelain that she was shining for her china cabinet. And then, before releasing them to wander over rug and tile again, she nuzzled my feet against her cheeks, planting a little kiss on each of them.

I thought she must be mad! Those feet were so *ugly!*

Oh, there were enough times when we definitely had to confront the oddness of my feet. Some of them will forever be remembered by her and me as our Saturday afternoon shoe trips. As frustrating as these desperate odysseys into the "special" shoe stores of several counties were to Mom, my three sisters and my brother soon found one benefit of those days: they could always count on a McDonald's junk-out after the every-six-months fiasco was over and done with.

"The only thing we can possibly fit her in is an oxford," the salesperson sympathetically would always say as she shook her head at Mom staring down at my stockinged feet dangling from the chair. This collegiate-sounding "oxford" translated into a black and white saddle shoe which I learned to detest for its eternal presence in my wardrobe.

For years Mom assiduously called ("Hello, do you carry a triple-E in a girl's shoe well thank you anyway good-bye") and visited every shoe store with even a hint of a reputation for fitting less than normal feet, searching for something *other* than an oxford or a sneaker. But I don't remember her having any luck for the first ten years or more of my life.

So we all trooped into shoe stores far and wide, while salesperson after salesperson tried one of those bland shoes on my feet, Mom trying to cheer me up with, "Now, that doesn't look so bad, Bobbie, and would you like a milkshake or a Coke at McDonald's dear?" She joked and made light conversation all the way to the hamburgers and through the fries and by the time it was over, those shoes really *didn't* look half-bad at all.

Sparks breaking from the fog of memory; sobbing and yelping over my feet, my sticklike legs, my weird frame, the unfairness of it all! And Mom's angry voice from across the room:

"All right. Go ahead. Feel sorry for yourself all your life. Sit in that corner and cry your eyes out while your sisters are out in the yard playing without you. Go on, Miss Self-pityitis-Cepko."

Had a bouncy ring to it.

And another time: Same selfish brat wailing through a hard day, but this time Mom is there, aching to soothe me, straining to hug my head to her chest, brushing my hair with worn hands, while I pull away, trembling with bitterness, annoyed at her sympathy and gentleness, wanting not to be comforted but to vent my rage at the person most vulnerable, the one who loved me most.

And she struggled to articulate that which we both knew could not be understood:

"I don't know why, Bert. I don't know why it had to be you. I wish you'd just *hate* me—take it all out on me if it would make you feel better. I don't *know* what I did to you." And soon she was crying, too, heavy tears plopping onto the top of my head.

I never believed it was Mom's fault.

But she was willing to take the blame if blame someone I must.

As only children can believe, I must have had a firm conviction that, if I grieved enough about my deformed feet and back, Mom would be able to find a way to change them into what they were meant to be. What a burden to lay on my dear mother—the albatross of impossible expectations. It is strange, though: I did not quite understand the connection between the surgeon Mom so often dressed me to visit, and the goal of "declubbing" my feet.

In *my* sight, those feet always looked more or less the same after each operation, just streaked with one more scar. yet in Mom's optimistic heart, each surgery represented hope that someday I would indeed walk "like everyone else," and that my leg muscles would build up to such strength that I wasn't so tired after a short walk. And for many years, until spinal problems reweakened my legs, we did walk side by side.

Yet Mom spent some of the best years of her life in pediatric wings of hospitals, entering on many an afternoon carrying a fresh box of crayons, leaving each evening with a bag of soiled laundry. One night before an operation, I was so frightened that Mom quickly arranged to have an extra bed wheeled in right next to mine. I still remember the overwhelming gratitude I felt just knowing she was there and would be walking to the operating room alongside my cart the next morning.

It must have seemed to Mom that when she wasn't driving to a hospital, she was on the road, lugging me to and from Annapolis to one of the kindest, most committed orthopedic surgeons in the medical establishment. These trips, like the non-oxford shoe hunts, were ones that Mom transformed into family adventures.

"Everybody got their swimsuits and towels?" I can still hear her double-check as we piled into the station wagon on many a stifling, muggy morning. We were going to the beach, and on the way we would stop by the doctor to line up an operation or to get a cast sawed off.

That's how she got *me* through it all.

How did *she* survive it all?

The most prominent image of my mother in my memory bank must be of her seated at her favorite tool of creating—her sewing machine—hands deftly guiding sleeve- or dress-shaped fabric under the whirring needle, foot gracefully resting on its heel while toes pumped the iron pedal. Through the years, her most relaxed face was directed at her "handwork" as she stitched on buttons, embroidered flowers onto the collar of one of our blouses, mended the torn knee of Russ's jeans or the ripped seam of Connie's nightgown.

Mom made just about everything we wore, Mary and I acting as her "twins" for whom she fashioned matching outfits. As we grew up, Mary and I were not to be caught dead in identical clothing, and none of us seemed to want to wear anything besides jeans and T-shirts. That's when Mom turned to quilting, setting the goal of bestowing a patchwork quilt upon each of us as we moved out of her house into our own separate dwellings.

Many evenings I came home to find her hunched over a project on our living room floor with boxes of her eclectic scraps tossed around her. She was framed by homemade templates of sandpaper or cardboard cut into tiny squares, triangles. Her "good scissors" (those we were not allowed to use on wrapping paper) were effortlessly shearing through a remnant folded many times over to get a multitude of pieces.

We have all received our quilts.

She's been intensely dissatisfied with each of them, pointing out the miniscule imperfections peculiar to each dazzling creation. As we held them up to praise and admire at birthdays and Christmases, none of us ever searched for, or even found these irrelevant errors.

For my sisters and my brother, as well as myself, dropped stitches in the fabric of life made no difference. She had taught us well.

Roberta Cepko · 59

Conversations at All Hours

1
o dead father
do you know
I am a decade older
than you were when you died

ten years beyond you

the grey springs from my scalp
vivid as wires
that pick up intimations in all weathers

my nerves sing high-pitched, tuneless

and sometimes now
they sing of death

2
they tell me
when you died
I cried

and would not leave the place above which
you had soared:
Heaven a hole in the blue canvas
over palms and pounded coral

until they told me you
would come too no matter
where I moved

since then I have dragged you
weightless frail balloon at the end
of a tether

where you might never have wished to go
on your own

and anchored you
in each new room
above the mirror on my dresser

3
they tell me
I wear your face

I do not know

in the snapshot
your head is thrown back
collar open at the throat
you are smiling

at your elbow my face
within the heavy fringes of hair
is tight as a peony bud
pink and petaled over

though not with pain

4
I wear the ring
you gave my mother
on the third finger of my right hand

clot of gold

its weight drags at my bones
holds me a little closer
to the earth's core

5
of the times you have loved me
of the times you have failed to love me
I have lost count

I have had the love
of one good man:
I did not think it enough

my hunger I keep wrapped in lilacs
and in the memory of lilacs

at times
I have thought I would die of it

6
gravid I have moved
with gestures as slow as though through water
as though I were the fetus
turning in the darkened fluid

I have borne you children: two:

they are strange to me
their faces open and jeweled
as day lilies

they believe that no one will ever leave them
without stopping first
to say goodbye

7
pulled down now
by illness

I scuttle and tack
black crab among fronds
on the floor of a murky ocean

I can not plan
on rising

Mary Grimley Mason ————————————————

The Bargain

I was born the fourth child in a family of two sisters, a year apart, a brother three years older, an in-residence grandmother, a father, a mother, and a fairly well-off establishment. I have very few early memories— mostly stories told me by my sisters and brother—mostly negative. The choosing of a name—Ruth, by my sisters—rejected by my mother. The slightly sadistic stories of pushing me around in my carriage, chanting "fat little Miss Stauffer." In short, no tales of admiring and enthusiastic siblings. I can't tell whether memory has been wiped away because of the traumatic illness of polio at the age of three or whether I simply have none.

I attribute the beginnings of night fears to my nightmares after returning from the hospital and finding I was unable to walk. Later, my fears increased, but I never thought of them as being a rejection of my "self" as an "incomplete" person, once suggested to me by a psychiatrist, who, discussing my "negative" image of myself, explained that I felt "alone with that awful person." I don't know if this was true, but I do know I developed many inner dialogues in my often solitary existence. Many of them with God, with whom I would make periodic bargains about getting well. It was rather like blackmail, such as you might use on a parent. "I'll hold my breath until you take away that food," or "I'll bite my arm until you let me go, too." The latter device I practiced but more as a self-punishment out of sheer frustration at inactivity. I didn't really want anything my parents could give me, but I did want something from God—to walk again and be as bouncy and free as my sisters and brother.

The most serious bargain I made with God was not for my own sake, however. It was for my grandmother when she was dying of cancer in our house at the age of seventy-six. Nana had been my constant companion and friend in my childhood. When the rest of the family would take off for a ski weekend in the Laurentians—banging around with long ski poles, my father growing more irritable until my sisters and brother exchanged the well-known look of fear and cowardice that develops under an irascible leader—I would remain on the upstairs landing looking down at them, sitting next to my grandmother's bedroom. She would be sitting in her rocking chair, sewing, her pincushion-round figure comfortably filling the chair, her white hair swept up like a puffy shower cap. She always seemed caught in a spell of serenity. When you entered her room, it was as if you crossed into a charmed circle around her where no human tensions could penetrate. She was always there, that is, most of the time, unless she went to visit her daughters, my aunts. She would look up, not say very much, but enough. Sometimes the twinkle would appear. That was one of her nicest gestures, a slightly ironic but benign comment on the world from the eyes. She was great at communicating this when my father exploded. The twinkle and a marvelous grimace of the lower jaw, saying, "Look at him. Beware the green dragon!" Only for a second. Then she'd resume an imperturbable poker face that said, "Who me? I didn't say a thing!" Occasionally she would become provoked when my father put on a dark hat and stood just behind the door as she entered the room—just to terrify her. He was a tease, and she always reacted with the desired gasp and "Elmer! Stop that." She was the only one who called my father by his christened name.

My bargain with God for Nana went like this. She had become ill, had been taken to the hospital against her wishes, had had an operation on her gall bladder, and had been returned home. I was eight years old at the time. The house was permeated with white nurses, low voices, the odor of the fatally ill. I knew she was not going to get better. Every day I would go in and sit beside the bed, holding for a moment the yellowing hand. Sometimes she had a Bible on the covers beside her; later, she was barely conscious or awake, but I would sit there and hold the ungrasping hand and think. Grief was not really known to me, but I knew that I could not lose Nana. Life could not be ordered or dealt with properly without her. God must know that. What did He want from me?

My communications with God were usually carried on from my bed at night, never at our church, the Presbyterian church down at the foot of the hill. I only play-acted my prayers and conversations with God in church. It was too difficult to talk when you had to think how you looked praying. I hadn't yet found the few Catholic prayers that one could say automatically, suspending consciousness of the world. A few streets up from our house in the Montreal suburb in which we lived stood the large Catholic cathedral of Saint Joseph's, an alien and grotesque place of worship to our family. But its very pomposity, sitting at the top of Westmount Mountain, at the crest of three or four hundred steps, was a compelling sign that it might be a good place to contact God. I had been in it from time to time and had already tried to make a deal whereby my crutches would join the stacks of crutches and canes left there by the faithful after they had been cured. I had tried a number of bargains, from giving up sweets—I was overplump—to reading a whole chapter of the Bible each night, but nothing had worked out. But now, I reasoned, I would be asking for someone else. That should make a difference.

The first question was how to get there. It was not easy to convince someone that I needed to go to Saint Joseph's, and it was too far for me to walk. Walking uphill was difficult for me and anyway, my mother always felt she needed to account for my whereabouts and such an outrageous request would be inexplicable to her. Besides, secrecy was important. My problem was miraculously, I hoped, solved soon after by a visiting cousin from New Jersey to whom we had to "show the sights." Mother was just going to drive by the cathedral and take Jan on to the wax museum, which specialized in religious martyrs—a Catholic phenomenon that Mother did not seem to grasp in the setting of the museum. I chose my moment just as we paused in front of the massive set of steps, dotted with kneeling pilgrims.

"Let's go inside the cathedral and look at all the crutches and canes," I ventured.

Mother looked particularly incredulous and slightly offended. "Jan would not want to see that, would you, Jan?"

My cousin was nineteen, attractive, pleasant, slightly indifferent. I looked at her apprehensively, but was relieved when she said, "Oh, let's go in."

My first step was achieved. Now I had to get in front of the altar without too much obvious purpose and make my plea. While Mother and Jan were looking at the white and pink and blue statuary with disapproving appraisal, I stumped down to the front pew, my heart pounding with shame as I knew everyone would think I was praying for my own cure. I was given a religious medal on the way by a woman in black, her face circled in a dark kerchief. She spoke in French and looked curiously, perhaps compassionately at me. I smiled a ghastly false smile, took the medal and reached the pew. The message was brief. "Let Nana live and forget about my ever being cured and able to walk."

I hadn't really decided on my bargain beforehand, and I tried out a number of minor and major sacrifices. When the moment came, the words just tumbled out—in my mind, that is. I don't think I had ever consciously thought about whether my "cure" was physically possible. "Residual polio"—my father had taken me from doctor to doctor trying to push the boundaries of medicine and revitalize the dead nerves my disease had left. In his curious way, he was more unaccepting than I of the inevitability of living with what I had. I was weary of the quest, but I still held a scrap of hope in the miraculous. And here I was, giving it up! I was astounded at myself and caught my breath in surprise.

"Mary, let's go, dear." My mother and Jan had approached, and we went on our way.

The next few days were hard. I had forgotten to set a time limit on God's cure of Nana. So I could not know when I would know whether the bargain had worked. Every day before school I would check with the day nurse, who had just relieved the night shift.

"Is my grandmother any better?" I'd ask.

"No, dear," she said on Wednesday morning—I had made my bargain on Saturday. "Our patient is not too well today." Then she raised her eyes—she was a prim, starched lady—"It's all in the hands of God," she said.

Wow, I thought to myself. Does she know? Then I realized her expression had been a commonplace, like a comment on the weather.

The next afternoon I had swimming at the local YWCA. Mother would take me after school. I had a special lesson with the instructor and hated the damp, hot indoor pool. I could never get dry and could not leap out like other swimmers and run through the showers. It was January, cold and wet in Montreal—snow, slush, a seasonal thaw. I still had to dress in a heavy "Red River" outfit of blue wool coat, red knitted pullover leggings, a knitted tuque, and mittens. I was particularly hot from the struggle of loading on the winter clothes and when I went outside the cold bitter air turned the heat to a chill sweat. Mother had left me and had returned to pick me up. Her face looked crumpled when she came back. Something was wrong, I knew.

"Nana has taken a turn for the worse, dear," she said. We drove without speaking. Mother did not discuss things very much.

When I went in, I realized Nana was dead. The "turn for the worse" had been death. My father was home, though it was only four o'clock. The doctor and nurse were coming out of Nana's room with my father. He didn't speak to me, but his eyes were blurry.

I took off my heavy clothes in silence with Mother's help.

"When will there be a funeral?" I asked.

Mary Grimley Mason · 65

"Tomorrow." Mother patted my arm. "You'll stay home from school."

I went upstairs to my room, passing my grandmother's room at the top of the stairs. Just the nurse was at the door now. All the others were downstairs. It was the "in the hands of God" nurse. I wanted to avoid her if possible, but I couldn't slip by unnoticed, taking as I did a considerable time to get up the stairs. She stood in the doorway, her arms crossed and her hands grasping her elbows neatly. She smiled on me as I approached.

"She's in the arms of Jesus," she said, with honey in her voice.

I crashed around the corner, achieving my room. When I had closed the door and sat on my bed, I didn't even try to sort out my conflicting emotions—heart thumping, hands clammy, my breath short, my still damp hair clinging with a chill to my head.

"So, I *can* get better!" I said it out loud, and it was a sob. Then I pulled the pillow to me to smother the dull ache I felt in my heart.

Raymond Lifchez and Cheryl Davis ─────────

Living Upstairs, Leaving Home, and at the Moscow Circus

LIVING UPSTAIRS

When I was seven years old my family moved from Boston to Milton, Massachusetts. Although it coincided with the great outflux of Jews from Roxbury, and the simultaneous influx of Southern blacks, our relocation probably had less to do with that migratory phenomenon known as "white flight" than with my physical disability. The Jews of Cheney Street worried about their changing neighborhood, but my parents' greatest fear was that as I grew older and, therefore heavier, they would one day soon be unable to carry me up and down the stairs. They had reason to worry.

Our apartment building lay more than halfway up Cheney, a steep slope leading to the summit of Elm Hill. Until I was three, we lived in number 58 on the third floor. To reach our apartment, one climbed a full flight of exterior stairs and two more inside, making about forty-five steps in all. My mother and father slung me over a hip, or "sat" me on a crooked arm and then huffed and puffed the way up, a climb that left them increasingly weary and ill-tempered. I never surmounted my fear of being dropped, and my consequent fretfulness annoyed them, as if, even so young, I was supposed to appreciate their efforts. After four years of this routine, when it was time to think about sending me to school, my parents must have realized that they could not carry me down every morning and up every afternoon five days a week (to say nothing of taking me on Saturdays to Grandmother's house and on Sundays to Franklin Park). Accordingly, we moved next door to number 60, where we lived for two years on the second floor. There, my parents had to contend with only four exterior steps and one flight inside: an improvement, relatively speaking.

For me, the move next door changed nothing. At an age when my peers were allowed to run downstairs to play with their friends, I depended on the willingness of my parents to "lug me up and down" (their phrase). When they carried me, I felt myself to be, in the most literal sense, a burden. I knew I tired them out. I resented their fatigue, for they groaned, as if insisting I admire their martyrdom on my behalf. I had one flight less of complaining to listen to, but I was still a captive audience and while, up and down the block, I saw children who were free, insofar as seven year olds are free, I was not.

After seven years of climbing hill and stair, my parents accepted the inevitable, and we moved to Milton, first renting for two years, then moving into our own home. My parents took me along on some of these house-hunting expeditions. They claimed they wanted it to be easier to carry me in and out of the house, not that they wanted me to be able to get myself in and out of the house. (I am not sure that they would have understood the difference between these two objectives.) Many of the houses seemed to my childish eyes to be nothing *but* stairs. I looked at those stairs and, sensing that this was critical, made my opposition to these prospective homes as relevant to my parents' way of looking at them as I could manage. Thus, I never pointed out that I couldn't get myself in and out; I reminded my mother of the last time she had strained her lower back carrying me up the steps. The one they finally purchased was far from a model of accessibility (we didn't then know the word) as can be imagined; yet it was superior to several they had considered.

The new place on Houston Avenue was a two-family house, with a first floor apartment six steps above grade. The lower unit had only two bedrooms, which meant, if we occupied it, that my sister and I would have to share a room. Three years older than I, Karen wanted her privacy; on this she was quite vocal. The upstairs unit offered access to several additional rooms in a finished attic. My sister could have a lot of privacy up there; I would have to crawl up yet another flight of stairs to invade her personal space.

My parents explained the options, as they saw them. Either we could have fewer stairs for me (and less space for the family), or we could have "a few more steps" for me (and ample space for the family, as well as a sister who wouldn't hate me for making her share a room). Then they said to me, an eight-year-old child, *"You* decide."

I should decide? What was going on here? What were they asking of me? I was eight years old; who was I to say where we should live? If I said, "Downstairs," they might go along with it—and then complain about and forever resent the fact that I had "made" them live in quarters too tight for comfort. They might *not* go along with it, and then I would see what I suspected was in fact the case: that they had already made the decision to live upstairs, that the choice was false. If I said, "Upstairs," my parents would love me, congratulate each other for parenting such a "mature" child, and, most importantly, be able in good conscience to answer any complaint about the stairs I might make in future years with the response, "But the decision was *yours*; we gave you the choice." So with an air of, "We only want what you want, dear," they ostensibly left it to me to determine where we would live. Feeling that I had been manipulated, without at the time being quite able to explain how, and feeling that I had no choice but theirs, I said, "I want to live upstairs." They praised my maturity, and I knew that, in some important way, I had been had.

My parents compounded still further the bind in which they had placed me when they asked me if I wanted a ramp up to the porch on the first floor. They pointed out that it would enable me at least to go from the driveway to the level of the porch, some forty-two inches above. "Still," my mother added, almost as an afterthought, "you'll still have the flight inside to cope with, so it doesn't really offer so much, does it?"

"No," I thought, "but if we had occupied the lower-level apartment, it would have got me right inside." I knew what my parents wanted me to decide. They reminded me how terribly expensive a ramp was and how hard my father worked and how little income the family had and how much my last stint in the hospital had cost. . . . Again, it was not hard at all for me to make a "mature" decision, one that I privately resented but for which I had ostensibly no cause to complain. After all, my choice had been "freely made."

LEAVING HOME

I left home when I was twenty-two years old. I would like to say that my reasons for leaving were the same as anyone of my age, but it wouldn't be true. "I want my independence," everyone says when moving out on their own, but what it meant for me as a disabled person was not quite what it meant for an able-bodied woman. It was not merely that I wanted to be closer to my job, or that my parents were putting a damper on their daughter's sexual activity (the absence of which was then so total that I regarded myself as nearly neutered). I left because I envisioned myself living with aging parents possibly for the rest of my life, simply because I feared to find out whether or not I could take care of myself.

I lived and quarreled with my parents in an inaccessible home, unable to get in and out unaided. I couldn't afford a car: Father was always reminding me how expensive "under-25" insurance was and expressing doubts that I could get a wheelchair in and out of a car myself, despite my telling him that I had, in fact, done it. (It never occurred to anyone to equip the family car with hand controls.) Taxis were financially disastrous alternatives, and obviously, I couldn't get a wheelchair on a bus. I went places if and when my parents were willing to drive me; they drove me everywhere I wanted, as long as I wanted what they wanted.

My mother believed that I couldn't minister to my own bowel care needs without her; she had convinced me, too, for a long time, but I was beginning to question this. The idea that she might be mistaken was intensely disturbing. It seemed as if she needed to feel needed so badly that my independence would be sacrificed. I was coming to resent her participation in my care as a gross and humiliating instrusion on my body, as an assault to my spirit. In the most basic physical sense, I had no privacy and I felt as if I were being repeatedly violated.

Suffice it to say we did not get along. Our household was perpetually engaged in an undeclared civil war. The only way to break the Gordian knot of our conflict was for someone to leave or die. Until I convinced myself that I might be able to live on my own, the only way out I could see was suicide. I was beginning to think of it continually, and it terrified me. When I realized that anything had to be better than this, I finally found the courage to plan the move.

Eventually, my parents realized that I was right; I had to go. My relatives were astonished that they would "let me go," as if it were their duty to compel me to stay. In reminding them that I was a reasonably intelligent adult, my mother reminded herself. Before too long, my parents (with who knows what internal conflicts) were helping me to look for an apartment.

As a low-income wheelchair user (salary of a junior secretary), my requirements for a dwelling were quite specific. The rent had to be $125 or less. The place had to be within a few blocks of Boston University, where I worked, since I was determined to push to the office, except in bad weather, when I would have to pay for a cab. (Incidentally, cabs were very hard to get for such short runs, since the drivers thought the effort of getting my wheelchair in and out was not adequately offset by the low fare. In winter, I would wait for up to an hour.) I had to be able to enter the apartment unaided and be able to maneuver in the kitchen and bathroom. Realtors told us only the size, the location, and the rent; therefore, we had to run around to all prospective apartments, a colossal waste of time.

This was 1967, and most of the buildings in Boston's Back Bay were hopeless. None of them had accessible front entrances. Most landlords refused to rent to me, saying, "What the hell do you think I'm running, a nursing home?" Finally, Mr. Greenblatt rented me a basement studio near

Kenmore Square and let my parents pay to have the back door ramped, "conditional upon the approval of the other tenants." Success! Let me describe this palatial abode.

To get to the rear entry, I had to push down an alley running between a nightclub-disco-bar and a movie theater. The alley, which had about a one-in-eight gradient, culminated in an expanse of fractured blacktop and loose dirt, which was deeply rutted and pocked by water-filled holes. I would never lose my fear of falling into them. I wasn't afraid of getting wet; I was petrified of being unable to get back into my chair in such a lonely spot, since the place was alive with rats. These weren't just any rats; they were Back Bay rats, enormous, sleek, and fearless. In daylight they stood in your path and watched you approach, as if appraising your edibility. The route disgusted me, but it led to the only semi-affordable, partially accessible place I could find in the area; therefore, in the absence of choice, I suspended judgment.

Inside, the studio was wood-paneled and dim. Some of the darkness was caused by the filth on the windows, the outside of which were uncleanable, because the burglar screens bolted onto the frames. A front burner on the stove didn't work and, since I couldn't reach the rear burners, it necessitated my cooking one-dish meals until I bought a hotplate (Mr. Greenblatt never did repair the stove). Although the bathroom door was wide enough, I had to remove it, since it blocked access to the tub; this was all right for me, but I thought it would disconcert any company I might have.

My parents let me take several pieces of furniture, some dishes and glassware, and their apprehensive blessings for the new venture. They moved the furniture in for me, cleaned the place up, and got a carpenter to build a ramp, under which the rats subsequently made a fine home of their own. I could see that my parents were far from pleased with the place. I wondered if they thought I liked it or hated it. This, my first apartment, was small, dark, roach-infested, hard to get around in, and surrounded by an army of vermin, but I loved it. It was *mine*. The door had a dead-bolt lock, and I could have all the privacy I wanted.

That first night, as my parents left me at my apartment, they assured me that I could call them any time of day or night; I had only to say the word and I could come home. I thought they were hoping my independence would be temporary, but I realize now how anxious they must have been. I've seen the same pattern when disabled friends leave home. I must say, my mother could hardly have been reassured when I asked her, "How do you know when water's boiling?" To everything they said, I nodded and answered yes. Yes, yes, yes. They knew I could hardly wait for them to leave.

The next morning was Sunday. I awoke at nine and lay there in bed, blissfully surveying my books, clothes, couch, walls, floor, ceiling, and door, luxuriating in my splendid squalor. I could let people in or not. I could buy the food I wanted, eat when I wanted to, go to bed or stay up when I wanted, go out when I wanted . . . *I* would choose. I didn't have to come home early because my parents didn't like to stay up late. I didn't have to ask my father to drive me anywhere. I could experience whatever presented itself, without asking my parents if it was all right with them. That was real independence. I thought of all that freedom and the new life I had begun. As I threw back the covers—I remember as if it were this morning—an incredibly wide grin stole across my face.

AT THE MOSCOW CIRCUS

I was excited to learn that the Moscow Circus was coming to Boston. Perhaps I was moved by nostalgia; many years ago, I had seen a pair of Russian dancing bears perform on the "Ed Sullivan Show" and I had never forgotten it. Besides, European circuses struck me as being much more fun than the three-ring American variety, which dazzled the eye but divided my attention. Whatever the reason, I was eager to go.

My life, at the time, revolved around disability. I was actively involved in several disability rights organizations and working for a state agency on a program to develop housing for low-income disabled people. I wrote, advised, consulted, and did research on disability-related issues. Sometimes it seemed as if I did nothing else. In a way, I think I looked at the circus as a chance to get away from it all. This was going to be an offnight for disability. No axe-grinding, no politicking. I would go back to worrying about civil rights and human services later. For one lovely evening, though, it would be cotton candy and Pavlov's performing dogs.

A circus is best enjoyed in company, so I invited two friends, Kent and Marsha. Kent bought our tickets, advising the ticket office that one of us used a wheelchair and that we wanted to sit together. Once inside Boston Garden, we traveled up several ramps and into an employee's elevator off the usual path of travel. My friends were shown their seats, which were several feet beneath the level of the aisle, while I remained in my wheelchair, since a transfer to the regular seat below was too difficult for me. With their heads at the same level as my footrests, conversation was awkward, but at least we were together.

More than six feet wide, the aisle left plenty of room, as long as I sat sideways, for people to pass me (my chair being less than twenty-three inches in width). The arrangement offered uncomfortable viewing, but I was willing to put up with it. The management, unfortunately, was less willing to put up with me. The usher, a rather self-important looking youth, advised me that "wheelchairs are supposed to sit over there," indicating a spot only slightly closer than Moscow.

"That's fine," I said, "but I'm with two friends who walk; they haven't brought their own chairs."

"You have to move; you're a fire hazard," he said.

"I'll move if you'll put folding chairs down there for my friends," I thought that sounded reasonable; Marsha and Kent seemed agreeable.

"Impossible!" he snapped. "I have other things to do."

"Then I'm afraid I can't move," I replied.

"Well," said the usher, "I'll let you stay, but the chief usher will be along soon. If you refuse to move for him, he'll throw you out; he won't be so nice." I wasn't aware he had been nice.

Inevitably, the chief usher materialized, a red-nosed, pudgy man of about sixty. I observed him reprimanding young children a few rows below me. He looked like a man who chose to vent his rage on everyone else's children because he didn't get any respect from his own. He enjoyed his authority as chief usher and he meant to use it. "You'll have to move," he fairly barked at me.

His bearing reminded me of my father, making me feel tiny, vulnerable, and very young. I actually trembled. Then I stiffened, enraged that he should treat me in this way. Why the hell should I move? We paid for these seats. I was here with my friends, and no one would separate us. "No," I quavered in a small voice.

Face purpled, the veins on his forehead stood out. He shouted, "I'm gonna get a policeman to throw you out," and left. I sat there shaking. My friends were angry but calm; I, in contrast, was intensely upset. They urged me to hold my ground and not permit him to bully me. What did that usher think this was, Kent joked, Russia? Despite my friends' support, I found the situation hard to endure. The ushers were making me feel as if I didn't have a right to see the circus with my able-bodied friends. They were wrong, I thought, wrong, but a small part of me was not so sure. I had spent twelve years attending a special school where I could be with what they said was "my own kind," and I wasn't always quite sure what my own kind was. Thus, I was easily intimidated. As the chief usher pointed a hostile finger at me, people had stared at us. The commotion embarrassed me, and although my rage demanded I stay, other feelings screamed at me to leave. Seeking a compromise, I noticed that I could, with difficulty, maneuver myself into the seats behind me. I asked a woman if she and her children would like to swap their seats for ours, which were more expensive and offered a better view. Suspicious at first, she traded gladly when I explained that it was probably the only way my friends and I could sit together. I think I also hoped that sitting in a regular seat would render me invisible.

While the chief usher summoned the law, I performed my own circus act in the stands. Dropping from my wheelchair to the floor, I crawled beneath the barrier, swung from it, and clambered up into a regular seat. Then I folded the wheelchair and brought it flush against the barrier. It now took up less than a foot of aisle space. Surely, I thought, the chief usher would be satisfied. I sat there regaining my breath, embarrassed to have had to crawl in public ("like a monkey," a relative used to say), but also feeling very capable, because of my improvisational use of the barrier to complete the transfer. Before my self-satisfaction had settled in, however, a policeman appeared. "That does it!" cried Marsha, "I'm calling my photographer friend at the *Boston Globe*." She and Kent sailed off in search of a telephone, leaving me alone with the law.

"Ma'am," he said softly, "I'm afraid you'll either have to move the chair, or leave." He was respectfully courteous, and I resolved to respond in kind.

"I'm not willing to sit apart from my friends," I said, "but I may be willing to park the wheelchair elsewhere, if it's in a safe place."

"You can park it over there," he said, indicating an exposed area. Anyone could steal it there, I decided. I wouldn't dream of positioning it out of close reach in an arena like this unless it were under lock and key and I told him so. "Why?" he asked gently.

"Would you leave your legs somewhere else?" I asked. "If my chair is stolen, I have no way of leaving this seat. It cost six hundred dollars, it's uninsured, and I can't afford a new one. I am a working person; if it's stolen, the state won't get me another. Without it, I can't work, shop, make dinner—or leave the Garden. Do you really want me to park it there?"

"But your chair is a fire hazard. You have to move."

I looked around us. From higher up in the stands, about twenty people dissatisfied with their seats had trickled down to sit in the aisles, on the stairs, anywhere they could. If any people were creating a potential hazard, they were, not me. "If you make me move, Officer, that would be discrimination." He clucked his tongue and drummed his fingers, impatient and annoyed. "Do you see all those people sitting in the aisles?" I asked. He did. "Well, if you make me move, without making all of them move, that's discrimination."

Puffing out his cheeks, he lifted the bill of his cap, then expelled the air. Cheeks deflated, he looked depressed. "I'm sure not going to be the one to make you move," he said, as he walked away. The chief usher returned just then, and so did my friends. The old man began to hector and bully me afresh. I had resisted all efforts to move for nearly an hour. The circus had been going on for half an hour and I hadn't seen any of it. I was tired, angry, and humiliated, and suddenly all I wanted to do was leave. Without even looking at the old man, who continued to shout, I told my friends I was tired and wanted to leave; did they mind?

As we rose from our seats, a little girl in a wheelchair entered, escorted by her mother and a girlfriend. She was crying, and from her mother's words, it was clear that she too had been told that she had to "sit with the wheelchairs," apart from her mother and friend. I was appalled. The little girl and I weren't the first people who had had trouble here. I remembered the experience of my friend Vivienne, who had come here with her five-year-old daughter. They had taken Viv's wheelchair away and forgotten to return it. As the Garden was closed and cleaned up for the night, she had sat marooned in the stands for an hour, her child clinging to her in tears. The memory of that little girl in the wheelchair preyed on me for a long time.

One more thing happened that night. It's a pity O. Henry couldn't have been there to record it. On the way out Kent went to the ticket office to demand our money be returned to us. He was advised that this performance was a fundraiser; no refunds were ever made for benefit performances. Where were the proceeds going? They went, Kent was told, to the Muscular Dystrophy Association "to help the handicapped."

Leslie A. Donovan —————————————————————

Recurrences

Twenty years now and still
my life lies close as garlic
about my neck warding off nightmares
of receding white walls,
institutional ceilings and the click
of bed rails snapping into place.

There are times even now when
the only thing that comforts me is
the feel of starched bed sheets about my head,
stark shadows on the walls beside me
and I can't swallow without felling
the lump left by the tracheotomy.

In my back, a metal rod won't let me
bend like Scarlett O'Hara into your arms
and the nerve endings in my thigh
never know the feel of your fingers
stroking it though
I pretend otherwise.

I Met Florence in Room 43

"We have another M.S. patient in the room;
We thought you might like to visit."
Well, why not. Think of the possibilities.
The curtain was pulled and I paused,
Left out. I found daring enough to ask
if she needed the space
And she pushed it back.

We shared.
M.S. job losses, plasma reactions
Drunken first husbands, fine daughters,
Strong second men.
Laughter over:
Legs slammed in doors,
Dropping pans, car swerves,
First "mortal" decrees from M.D.'s,
The leanings toward suicide,
Limb pain, and fatigue.

The drunken loudness in our chatter
Was silent when she left.
I watched a student from Nigeria
Strip and scrub her bed.
He didn't have M.S.
And was embarrassed by the manual chores he did
While I envied each move he made.
I missed her crusty company;
I miss her now.

Marsha Saxton ────────────────────────────

"I'm on a Lot of Committees":
An Interview with Frances Deloatch

Marsha Saxton: *What was it like for you to grow up in an institu-tion?*

Frances Deloatch: Well, that's all I ever knew. When I went home, it was mostly for the weekends or for holidays, if that. Because I broke a lot—broke my bones a lot—and also because it was hard for my family to take care of me because of where they lived. And it was okay. It wasn't like some kids who go into an institution and then stay home for a long time. For me that's all I really knew. And I made a lot of friends there. The nurses, when I was younger, treated me totally different in the hospital. I wasn't there because I was sick. I was there because I had a cast on or because it was the only place I could go at the time. So they would let me help them with the kids. When they were busy, you know, they didn't have time to play with one of the kids. Or if they needed help changing a kid's bed, they would say, "Here, Frances, you hold the kid while we change the bed."

MS: *So, you were part of the staff.*

FD: Yeah, sort of, yeah. They would let me run errands for them. And then when I did go home, though, I really didn't do much, except stay and watch TV. Because we always lived on second or third floors, my dad working all the time, no one else in the family driving, so mostly once I got home, I would stay home until it was time for me to go back. So in one sense, being in the hospital at that time was more fun than being at home.

MS: *What do you feel like you missed, being in an institution for most of your childhood?*

FD: I missed being home with my brothers, being home with my fam-ily. I think because I stayed in institutions I'm a lot different than they are. . . . I have second cousins and first cousins that my brother relates better to. My brother communicates with them more than I do. I don't think they even really know me anyway. I don't go out and socialize with them and things like that, the way my brothers do. And I think that's all because

---

Note: This interview appears in the forthcoming Feminist Press film tentatively titled *Breaking Silences,* directed by Midge MacKenzie (Film Boston). This excerpt is taken from the interpreter's transcription.

I was in institutions and they didn't get to know me, they didn't get to know that it's okay, that a person in a chair can go out. So I missed just being around the family in general. It has gotten better because I've been out of the institutions a long time and living on my own. We'll go out to family gatherings, but my mom is still a little bit overprotective of me.

MS: *How about being black and disabled in the institutions? Were many of the staff black where you were?*

FD: Actually, for the last couple of years I've been having a total battle against myself and the institutions I've grown up with. There were black children, but they were mostly either younger than I or they were sick so they weren't able to really communicate. And there weren't that many black staff. So . . . although I am black, I sort of grew up in a white man's world. And I think I have a hard time dealing with my family beause of that. I grew up around white people, and most of my friends are white. That's the culture I grew up in. . . . My family has a hard time understanding why I'm the way I am, which is physically black but emotionally and the way I think a lot of times, white. And I think they have a hard time knowing, understanding why that may be. It's like, I have to deal with two cultures at once.

MS: *What was it like for you when you first moved out on your own?*

FD: Real scary. I had to get used to it. I had to train myself to know when it was time to eat, that you eat three meals a day—I had to train myself to think that way. What time my appointments were. I never carried a calendar book in my life up to when I started moving out on my own. I had to get used to all of those adjustments, the typical everyday skills. How am I going to deal with people staring at me? How am I gonna deal with people's attitudes about the disabled? Some people think they still should be in institutions. At the schools, we were all disabled, but when you're out on the street, when people look at you, do I respond to it? Do I ignore it? Do I try to educate, or what? I had to learn what to do with all that. How to protect myself.

MS: *Once you moved out into your first apartment, what was it like?*

FD: I heard every noise in the book. Because, you know, when you're in a hospital or in your home, either you have brothers or a roommate or something. This was on my own. I didn't have anybody. So the first couple of nights I was like, ooh, what's gonna happen, you know? Someone's gonna come in. I made sure I locked the door. But then I got used to it, and I've been living there six years and I really like it. The people out in the street aren't as scary to me in terms of the way they're thinking. Well, some of the weirdos you see out in the street, they used to really scare me. I used to hate passing by them. Because I'd never know what they're going to do, and now I just pass right by them, and if they make any sort of comment, I just ignore it.

MS: *What were some of the choices, the first choices that you made that felt like important symbols of being on your own?*

FD: Let's see. Well, I went to a club and movies—R-rated movies, I went shopping by myself, I went to the beaches. In the hospitals, if they let you, it's more structured. Where like five nurses go, too. I don't have to do any of that anymore. Come and go as I please.

MS: *I know issues that you and I both share as disabled women concern reproduction and parenting. Can you talk some about what that's like for you, wanting to have children with your disability?*

FD: Well, first I want to tell you what my disability is. It's called osteogenesis imperfecta, which means that the bones are fragile, and makes you small for your age. I'm twenty-eight, but I'm only 3'3". And that's one of the reasons why I cannot have children. It's been hard, emotionally, a lot. Because of the fact that I see kids all the time, and also because I'm the type of person who . . . would make a good mother. I've always worked with kids. And to see kids a lot, it's like, you see 'em but you know you can't have 'em, and all your friends are having kids, and friends of friends are having kids. So a lot of times I get depressed about it. Especially while I'm working with them. And then you sort of get into fantasizing about what it's like to have a child.

MS: *What are some of the things you've gone through, realizing that you can't have children?*

FD: When I was a kid I always thought that I would be a mother. And I would take care of a child. And then when I was about eighteen, nineteen years old, I sort of knew, but I had that denial type of thing. And I would still say, one day I would get married and have a child. So one time I went to a hospital and this doctor talked to me about having a child, and I was asking him some questions. And he said, "You know that you'll never be able to have a kid, because you're small and the kid may not live through that or you either." I didn't know what to say for awhile. And I just left sort of in shock. I didn't know whether to ask questions. In the institution at bedtime, I was in bed thinking, and I just, you know, started crying, and I still didn't tell anyone what was wrong. Because I was still sort of denying it. Saying, ah, he's wrong, he's wrong. I also realized that it was the first time I ever really hated my disability. I've gone through the broken bones, I've gone through the hearing loss. And I'd survived that. You know, I figured I'd pick myself right back up. But then, when someone tells you you cannot ever have something that you really want, then it was like, why, why was I born with disability?

MS: *What are your options in relation to children?*

FD: I can adopt. I think. I mean, I know I'd like to one day. But . . . I feel it's gonna be hard. Because although the laws say they can't discriminate, try to tell social workers that. I feel that I'm really going to have a tough battle on my hands if I decide to adopt. The other thing . . . I'm going through is, do I want to be married? On the one hand, I do because I really feel that I'd want my child to have a father, but on the other hand I say, do I want to go through the hassle of getting married? . . . But, I also see that it would be hard to handle a child without someone else helping me out. You know, picking up and that type of thing. One thing I definitely have decided, and I'm coming to this conclusion more and more, is that I want to make my life career working with kids. Although it's hard for me to work with them, I feel that I'd probably be worse off if I didn't. And a lot of times you can fantasize that you're a mother or whatever to somebody. So I think I'm better off doing that. But it'd be real hard.

MS: *How about being black, female, small, hearing impaired—how do you think that combination affects you?*

FD: I'm on a lot of committees. It's like being all minorities in one. That's basically what I am. I'm hearing impaired, black, a woman, disabled. A lot of times I'm asked to be on committees, and I don't know whether they're trying to kill two birds with one stone, you know, because they have to have so many blacks or so many women or so many people with chairs, so many hearing impaired, or whatever. So, a lot of times I think, well, do they really want me for me? Then, on the other hand, I find it kind of challenging, because I *am* all those minorities, and because I can sit there and say, well, you can't discriminate against me because I am black, or you can't discriminate against me because I am hearing impaired. It's a challenge to see what people will or will not try to get away with.

MS: *Does one of your disabilities seem like the worst?*

FD: Okay, when I was younger, I didn't have the hearing impairment. That comes because of the osteogenesis imperfecta. It only comes as you get older. So, I didn't really know about the hearing impairment until was about seventeen. And even then that did seem to be a little worse than the fact that I broke bones. I like to talk on the phone, and I like to talk to people. And so when I found out I was hearing impaired, it seemed like it'd be even worse than broken bones because it's my communication system. How would I talk on the phone? When I did go home that's what I would do, because there's nothing else to do. So, I thought, oh great. How would I work with kids? Could I work with kids with a hearing impairment? I would probably have to learn another way of communicating, which I did. I did learn sign language. So just that whole thing was going through my mind. Then I would have to wear a hearing aid, which was also was like, great, then it'll be really evident that I have another disability. So I went through that whole stage of not wanting to wear the hearing aid. But if I didn't wear it, I couldn't hear. And even now I'm supposed to wear two. But I don't wear the other one, first of all because it doesn't do any good anyway, but second of all where I work with kids, I don't want people to think I'm more disabled than I really am.

MS: *You said you sign. Do you feel a connection to the deaf community?*

FD: I have, yeah. I've gotten closer to the deaf community. I know people who are deaf and hearing impaired, I've gotten involved in some of the agencies of the hearing impaired and deaf. Because now that I am hearing impaired, there's a lot of things that I need so that I can live independently. Like a volume-controlled phone. When I don't have a hearing aid on, at night, I need things like flashing lights for the doorbells, and fire alarms, things like that. So, I've had to deal with those kinds of equipment. And again, I'm more involved being on some of their advisory boards. And also using interpreters in some situations, not all. If I go to big conferences or meetings, where I know the room's gonna be hard to hear in, or where I know people have low voices, I will tend to use an interpreter. I've only been doing sign language for three years, so I'm still new at it in a lot of ways. I use interpreters not only for the signing, but also to help if I don't hear something. At least I can ask the interpreter if I missed a word or something. Also, I think mentally I'm sort of trying to prepare myself so that if I do go totally deaf, I'll be ready.

MS: *Your advocacy and community work, tell me more about that.*

FD: I do like the people. I like giving suggestions and helping in that sense, the best way I can. So I'm on the advisory board for Massachusetts Office of Deafness and the advisory board for the Office of Handicapped Affairs. Things like that. And I get asked to do a lot of disability awareness with school children, which, out of everything, has to be one of my favorite things to get asked to do. Because I think it's important to hit them when they're young. They get a lot of stereotypes from their parents. So I try to break that right away, while they're in first grade, third grade, or whatever. And I also do it with medical students, which I also feel is important for the disabled community. I give them some of my experience in terms of the breaking bones, but I also tell them they're gonna learn some disabilty stuff as well, and I'm not talking about the medical stuff. I'm talking about how to advocate for us or learn to treat us like people.

MS: *Was there a particularly bad experience that you had in a medical setting?*

FD: One that I have to say was the weirdest—it wasn't real bad-bad, but it was when I was about seventeen years old, and I had just had surgery on my leg. I was in the hospital room and all these doctors came in. The next thing I know they're whipping off my covers without even saying anything, asking me anything, or saying "How are you doing?" I would have to say that that's the most degrading thing that I think anyone could ever do. I mean it's bad enough when you're young and have that happen to you, like five or six years old. But it's even worse when you're seventeen, and these are a bunch of guys and they didn't even have the courtesy to ask—I just thought that was so insensitive. And I think it was after that that I started to say, okay, I'm going to start setting limits and saying no. I became really good at asking doctors what they want. And saying to them, well, no, I'd prefer not. I became really good after that. I felt that I had to or else they were going to keep on doing that.

MS: *So you demand their respect.*

FD: That's all I think that a lot of people want. Whether they're disabled or not, I think it's just a matter of wanting respect. And I don't think that's too much to ask.

Barbara Ruth

Recovery Poem #4

Now, when I think of making love with you
It's your fingers on my face I crave
The slow, sweet strokes
The tenderness.
It's the time
When you put your hands around my belly
Holding my incision
And cradling me to sleep
That I remember
The way you healed me
Made me feel safe
Against your skin
So woman soft.
And when I think of making love
Now it is your gentleness
I remember
And I crave.

Debra Kent ————————————————————————

In Search of Liberation

When I joined a women's consciousness-raising group a few years ago, I'm not quite sure what I expected—to discover some bond of understanding with the other women, perhaps, to feel myself part of the growing sisterhood of the liberation movement. But through session after session, I listened in amazement and awe as the others delivered outraged accounts of their exploitation at the hands of bosses, boyfriends, and passersby. They were tired of being regarded as sex objects by male chauvinist pigs. All their lives, they lamented, they had been programmed for the confining roles of wife and mother, roles in which their own needs were submerged by those of the men they served.

I had to admit that their indignation was justified. But it was impossible for me to confess my own reaction to their tales of horror, which was a very real sense of envy. Society had provided a place for them as women, however restricting that place might be, and they knew it.

Totally blind since birth, I was seldom encouraged to say, "When I grow up I'll get married and have babies." Instead, my intellectual growth was nurtured. I very definitely received the unspoken message that I would need the independence of a profession, as I could not count on having the support of a husband.

For myself and for other disabled women, sex discrimination is a secondary issue—in life and in the job market. To the prospective employer, a visible handicap may immediately connote incompetence, and whether the applicant is male or female may never come under consideration at all. In fact, the connotations that disability holds for the public seem, in many ways, to negate sexuality altogether. In a culture where men are expected to demonstrate strength and dominance, the disabled man is regarded as weak and ineffectual. But in social situations he may have an advantage over the disabled woman.

Our culture allows the man to be the aggressor. If he can bolster himself against the fear of rejection, he can make overtures toward starting a relationship. At least he doesn't have to sit home waiting for the telephone to ring.

According to the stereotype, women are helpless creatures to be cuddled and protected. The disabled woman, however, is often merely seen as helpless. A man may fear that she will be so oppressively dependent upon him that a relationship with her may strike him as a terrifying prospect. To prove him wrong she may strive for self-sufficiency, only to have him say that she's too aggressive and unfeminine.

People may pity the disabled woman for her handicap, or admire her for her strength in overcoming it, but she is too unlike other females to be whistled at on the street. Somehow she is perceived as a nonsexual being. If men don't make passes at girls who wear glasses, what chance does a blind girl have, or one in a wheelchair, or a woman with spastic hands?

American culture still pictures the ideal woman: slender, blonde, blue-eyed, and physically perfect. Of course, there is plenty of leeway, and not every man is worried about these cultured stereotypes when choosing a mate. But as long as a woman remains a status symbol to the man who "possesses" her, the living proof of his prowess, the woman with a disability will be at a severe disadvantage. The man who is not completely secure will be afraid to show her off with pride because she is too different.

The worst period for most disabled men and women is probably adolescence, when conformity to the group's norms is all-important. Then, even overweight or a bad case of acne is enough to brand one as a pariah. Things may become easier later on, as emphasis on outward appearances gradually yields to concern with qualities as well. But it is hard to shake off the sense of being an outcast.

Even when she establishes a healthy relationship with a man, the disabled woman may sometimes find herself wondering, "Why does he want me unless there is something wrong with him? If someone else comes along, won't he leave me for her?"

But why, I ask myself, should it ever make a difference to society whether people with disabilities are ever accepted intact—as human beings with minds, feelings, and sexuality? Though we have become more vocal in recent years, we still constitute a very small minority.

Yet the Beautiful People—the slender, fair, and perfect ones—form a minority that may be even smaller. Between these two groups are the average, ordinary citizens: Men who are too short, women who are too tall, people who are too fat or too thin, people with big noses, protruding ears, receding hairlines, and bad complexions. Millions of people go through life feeling self-conscious or downright inadequate, fearing that others will reject them for these physical flaws. Perhaps the struggle of disabled people is really everyone's battle against the binding rules of conformity, the struggle for the right to be an individual.

As I sat in that consciousness-raising group, I realized that disabled women have a long and arduous fight ahead. Somehow we must learn to perceive ourselves as attractive and desirable. Our struggle is not unlike the striving for self-acceptance of the millions of nonhandicapped who also fall short of the Beautiful People image.

Our liberation will be a victory for everyone.

Debra Kent · 83

Deborah Kendrick ————————————————————

For Tess Gallagher

Once the spell has broken,
The room no longer wrapped in your reading,
My friend introduces us.
Seized by a lapse into old reactions,
I see clearly laid out before me two alternate routes
For this sliver of human relating.
Fantasy skims smoothly over one,
While masochistic reality creates the other.

In my mind's eye we talk
Of line and phrases and meter.
Conversation spilling into the night, we walk
And share a glass of wine;
We laugh like conspirators, over children,
Pets, and lovers we have known.

But here, in the tomblike reality of truth,
I scramble for the spoken syllables,
Deny my claim to our shared muse,
And know that the moment's direction is permanently, pathetically cast.

I am aching to tell you
How I loved your coat and your hug and your black porter.
But I have chosen my fork
And it is too difficult to go back.
Drawing my real and imaginary shutters,
Restraining the light from escaping into my face,
I know I have sealed our course.
All we talk about instead
Is the only
Other
Blind person you have known.

Incidental

He is new to her, he's seen her
  at concerts, he asks her out
for sea food, they end up at
  the beach where she stumbles
on her crutches over muddy
  stones, weeds, as he moves quietly
beside her, watching, making no attempt
  at talk
Back in his car she looks
  away at the dark sweet-smelling
water glistening on the stones
  while he plays a tape of
Bach transcribed for classical
  guitar, a slow sad prelude
She stretches
  the bad leg and lets her eyes
drop to his hand
  on the stick shift, lit
by the glow of Bach and dashboard,
  and to his thighs
in their tailored
  jeans and remembers
how he carried her up the restaurant
  stairs and set her down, casual,
as if she were a child

Miriam Ylvisaker ─────────────────────

Significant Others

At night, when Laura has trouble sleeping—too many voices grabbing hold, bringing shards of the past, knots and chunks of the present—she amuses herself by shuffling pieces, trying new slots, different combinations, looking for better ways, hoping that some quick twist of the Rubik cube will let everything fall into place.

After a while inner speech lets go. She moves from words to images, grateful for dreams. She sees the mother cat living longer, sees herself walking down the road beside wild blackberry bushes and under live oak trees, sees herself moving easily and without fear in any landscape she might choose. Crocus bloom forever. Storms from previous dreams subside. She will not give up; everyone feels alone.

Time in days, like sleep at night, comes in fragments. She puzzles over what is worth keeping and what can, after all, be let go.

The women's group is a problem. Once in, it is hard to back out. Fortunately it is not a long-term commitment. Eight sessions, they agreed; then they would decide whether or not to continue.

Laura does not really like the other women in the group, their hopelessness and despair, their endless descriptions of mornings—figuring out how to get up, pulling themselves out of bed, rocking back and forth on their feet, falling back onto the bed again, trying once more, making it or not making it, having to call for help. She does not like looking at their knobby, deviated fingers, their fat ankles encased in bizarre, jerry-built shoes, does not want to watch the cautious way they move, as if pain made motion dangerous. She hates looking at them, hates looking at herself.

Nor does she really like Ellen, the group leader. Ellen has perfect knees and thin ankles, an easy way of slipping off her shoes, tucking and folding her legs beneath her on the couch, note-taking all the while, heavy leather binder balanced effortlessly on her lap. Laura would rather not listen to her advice. "Now and then allow the inner mother to take over, nurture yourselves. Develop tools to deal with limitations; do not let life back you into corners where your only choice is between the rock and the hard place."

Arthritis support groups are the latest thing. Laura understands the need but, my god, she thinks, how hard we work at it.

"How are you?" one woman asks another as they gather in Laura's living room.

"Fine, just fine," is the response.

"But what happened to your arm? Why is it in a sling?"

"Oh, just a little fall," Elaine replies.

On a trip with her husband, traveling up the coast, they stopped for lunch and Elaine slipped off a low restaurant counter stool, injuring her arm. Then she hurt it again while working in their daughter's tiny apartment kitchen. Now she holds the arm, bent at the elbow, immobile, cradling it against her as if it were an injured infant. Fingers, wrist, forearm, and elbow are massively swollen and covered with black, green, blue, and magenta bruises.

"It must hurt," Ruth says.

"Oh, not too much," Elaine replies, curving her lips upward, open slightly, in what appears to be a smile.

Ellen listens intently. She makes eye contact as people speak, her left hand resting, palm down, fingers spreading and closing on the silky fabric of her skirt.

Hazel bursts into jerky speech. "What shall I do? How shall I decide?" Multiple surgeries, prostheses, and orthotics have turned her into a stick figure. Hazel's legs stretch straight out in front of her, plastic braces run up along her calves, a foam rubber collar encases her neck. The orthopedist, young, eager, is experimenting with ankle implants; he does not guarantee success.

"Can I stand another operation?" she asks. "I doubt it, but how much longer can I stand this pain?"

Each woman has a different stance, a better idea. Try a new doctor, try imagery, try body work and realignment training. Feldenkrais or Rolfing, try Certo and grape juice, Chinese herbs, acupuncture, tai chi, homeopathy, gold injections, yucca powder, brewer's yeast, Dr. Dong's fish diet, the health spa in Willows.

"It's the fog," Ruth says, "It's so heavy these days."

"I know where you are coming from," Ellen says. She herself has had long-term illness; has been sick, intermittently, from age ten to thirty-five, when surgical discoveries made possible what seems to be permanent remission from her chronic bowel disease. Two marriages, one child, a Ph.D. in counseling later, she has determined to try to help others. She smokes incessantly, but she is a good listener, and she does not limit discussions. If someone wants to talk about their Oraflex rash or alternate sexual positions or how to cope with teenagers, she accommodates.

Audrey, who seldom speaks, says, "The other day my son said he had to talk to me. 'Mom,' he told me, 'I have to be honest. I want you to know that I'm gay.' "

Audrey weeps. Her son is thirty-five and has never married. That weekend her husband, who often drank too much, had challenged the son. "What's wrong with you? Where are your women? What are you, some kind of a fag?" It was the weekend Audrey had invited all the relatives for dinner. Her husband, who had promised to help, went out for groceries Friday afternoon and didn't return until Sunday morning, smelling of liquor.

"Is this a pattern from the past?" Ellen asks.

"Oh yes, often," Audrey says. "And each time I ask myself how I can stand it any longer. But then, how could I possibly leave? How could I manage without someone around? Besides, the truth is that I really do love him."

The women go on to talk about their husbands. Janice has just left hers, asked him to leave actually, says they never could really communicate; he was too repressed. Now she has taken a lover, but she says she cannot be sure, she does not feel attractive any more, what could he see in her?

"With this body how can I possibly be a good wife?" Hazel asks. "My husband is too nice to me. I don't deserve it. And then, I try not to think about it, but I can't help wondering," she adds, "is it possible that he is seeing someone else?"

Laura listens and says nothing. She feels left out by the women's stories of husbands, lovers, children—"significant others," as Ellen calls them.

Car doors are a real problem. Laura's seventeen-year-old two-door Valiant has pushbutton handles and heavy doors, easy enough to work when she bought the car, close to impossible now. She tries to remember to leave the door not quite latched shut, but yesterday, still angry, she must have given it a hard slam, for it is closed tight when she comes out to the car in the morning.

Using the handle of her cane she presses on the doorhandle button; cane slides, latch escapes. She repositions the slightly right-angled cane handle to give most leverage, holds as firmly as she can, presses again. The door opens and she pulls it till it holds. Once inside the car, to close, she reaches as far as she can, pulls. The door does not budge. She pulls harder, almost falls out. Putting one leg half out of the car she pulls the car door a bit closer, careful not to close it so much that it will snap her leg in its jaws. Leg back inside, reaching again, using both hands, she pulls hard, gives the door a slam, settles in.

She is due at the orthopedist's in San Francisco in half an hour and these maneuvers have used up way too much time. Even driving fast, it does not leave her the minutes she needs to get from the garage to the doctor's office. If the handicapped parking space is taken she will be in trouble.

What to do about the old car—junk it or fix it? "Don't spend another penny on repairs," the husband of a friend advises. "The whole front end is marginal." With its 150,000 miles, its dents and rust, its cushion stuffing popping through, this is not a classy car.

But mostly it runs, and Henry, down at the Chevron station, doesn't mind working on it. "It's not like the new cars," he says. "This one was meant to last a long time. Besides, when something goes wrong with it, it's not that hard to fix."

As she drives she plays with the idea of what to buy instead. She cannot work gear shifts with pushbuttons, in bucket seats she sinks below the vision line, keys on steering columns are hard to turn. Even if she had the money, even if she bought the latest model with all the extras—power steering and power brakes, automatic shift, power windows, cruise control—the car would still be stiff with newness. . . .

The window on the driver's side of Laura's car sticks badly after rain. She has not remembered to roll it down before leaving home. She struggles with it now as the Bay Bridge toll-taker waits, eying the cars backed up behind her. "Thanks *loads,"* he says, as she reaches him her quarters.

At the last women's group meeting Ellen's assignment was: "Make a list of significant others for next time. We'll share."

None of her business, none of theirs, Laura found herself thinking. Maybe I'll invent something. A husband, divorced when I was—how old?—twenty-two, maybe, or better yet, later on—thirty perhaps—so she could add to the list two children. A son at Stanford, a daughter who had just left home to live with friends in Boston.

"Dear Mother of the Year." Maybe, instead of making a list for Ellen, she'd write a letter and read it to the group. "I see the President has given you an award. I presume your having six children must have had something to do with it. I can assure you that, even though I have no children myself, I know as much as you do about . . ." She feels herself losing hold of the voice; she finds the hostility too hard to maintain.

One of Laura's two cats has just died. The cat, a black and white bobtail, was born in the spring of the year Robert Kennedy was assassinated. That was the spring Laura thought of herself as being in love with the principal of the school where she was then teaching. She pursued him: in the cafeteria in the morning, at lunch time, walking to the parking lot, once in a while going some place after school for a drink. He had a wife, Laura knew that, she had seen her: stylish, attractive, marcelled hair and pencilled eyebrows—pale, jittery, and classy looking at the same time.

After a time, whenever Laura looked she found him, as if he knew where and when she would be looking and was waiting for her. And she still believes it was only to her he said, "It is hard to find someone to really talk to." On that day they sat in the cafeteria drinking coffee. She studied his hands, the movements of the bones in his wrists, pattern of gold watchband on dark brown skin, square strong fingers wrapping themselves around his pipe. She tipped her saucer toward him so he could empty his pipe bowl. The tobacco, hardened, stuck, then loosened suddenly in a shower of small grains. He looked up at her and laughed; she laughed too. No one was watching. As she left to go to class he lifted one finger to graze her hand; the residual tenderness lasted all day.

"What do they expect me to do?" Jim asked one morning, standing in Laura's classroom, smashing his fist against the windowsill, looking down across the courtyard onto the charred roof of one of the portable buildings, fire-bombed over the weekend. Emboldened to reach out by the anguish in his voice, she said, "Why don't you come to my house after school for a drink. We can talk."

When she came home from school that afternoon she found that the mother cat had given birth to three kittens on the floor of her bedroom closet. The cat looked up at her, blinked, purred, then went back to her determined cleaning and nursing. "Come and see my kittens!" she called to Jim when he arrived.

They stood together in the narrow space of the closet door, bed behind them, looking down at the cats. His arm, palm against the door jam, circled above and behind. They turned toward each other; moments passed; nothing was said. Then somehow, by one or both of them, a decision was made and they moved apart and into the living room. He drank bourbon, they talked, but conversation was difficult, and he left soon.

Later, after Jim transferred to another school, someone told Laura he was having an affair with a blonde counselor "who," the person said, "looks a tiny bit like you." And later still she ran across someone who saw him now and then. "Is he still married? Is he happy?" she asked. "Yes and no in that order," was the response.

And just the other day she herself saw him, crossing the street by the post office, looking not so different from the past, a good spring still in his walk. She might have stopped to talk to him but did not. It was hard to judge the distance; she was not sure whether she could park and walk across the street fast enough, or if she did whether he would recognize her. To this day she does not know how he saw her back then, but she knows she does not want him to see her the way she is now.

"What do you want done with the body?" the vet asked on the phone. Laura was silent a long time.

She had not planned to keep the cat, but time passed and she was unable to give him away. "What's wrong?" people asked. "How come it doesn't have any tail?"

She had named the cat Bobby, but after Los Angeles and Sirhan Sirhan that did not seem cute any more, so for the rest of the cat's life he was Kitty or Baby or, sometimes, Goofy. Like his uncertain name he was an uncertain cat, fragmented, often sick, afraid of strangers, friendly only to Laura, frightened when she cried, purring when things went well. Dogs barking, skunk scent, roofers on the neighbor's house, firecrackers, and Halloween noise all prevented him from returning home; he hunkered down between the rock wall and the garage until long after danger was past.

"What choices do I have?" she asked.

"Well," he replied, "I am not squeamish about dead animals' bodies, but I really don't like what the county does with them. I prefer to send them up to a place called Bubbling Wells where they bury them. Not," he added, "individually, of course."

"In the ground?"

"Yes."

"Fine," she replied.

"Intermittent vomiting," was what she told him when she brought the cat in for treatment, but it had seemed constant. Part of a day and all through one night the cat retched and spit up, then, spasms finished for the moment, gulped enormous amounts of water. Toward morning, when it was beginning to be light, the cat stood at the door, miaouwing harshly in the way that said he was about to be sick again. She let him outside, watched shudders rack his body, pink liquid stain the sidewalk. Where once he sniffed, played with leaves, now he crouched, barely able to move; their eyes met in terror.

"I cannot get the toxicity down," the vet called to say after two days. "Kidney failure is common in old cats. If in this amount of time I have not been able to . . ." His voice trailed off. One of them mentioned euthanasia.

"How soon can it be done?" Laura asked.

"Within minutes," he replied.

She told herself it was foolish, but she mourned; it rained, she stayed in bed. I have lost the bobtail. The mother has lost her son. The bobtail is no more. She regretted not taking pictures, not noticing oftener how the cat moved, how he stretched, exactly how his markings went.

The bobtail was a difficult cat to get to the vet. He had become too heavy for her to lift, so she always had to find someone to help her catch and carry. Frightened, the cat would escape under the bed, behind the stove, until he was captured, fighting, scratching, dragged and forced yowling into the carrier. Perhaps, if, a few months ago when he was attacked by another cat, she had not delayed about taking him to the vet, the bite would not have become infected. Perhaps if he had not been weakened and vulnerable he would not have been attacked again, this time more seriously wounded in the chest. The cat has become part of Laura's list of "if onlies"—losses which can in no way be blamed on physical disability but which are, in every way, contaminated by it.

Rebecca Gordon —————————————————————

By Her Hands

What, you didn't ask this morning,
will happen to us
if my hands grow too
stiff, too weak to love you?

I shook but did not speak, afraid
to break the seal
your courage left intact
though words paced
restless in my chest:

We shall have still
a multitude of lips between us
and the will.

In quiet I remembered
with whatever skill she loves
a carpenter lives
by her hands

Later we shop. I watch you
choose a cup
a sister's birthday gift,

swift stung
grab your hands, kiss
at your knuckles
bent around the belly
of the cup they hold,
red and cold

a kiss for luck
a kiss for suppleness as if
to suck this stiffness out
through the fingertips.

Now outside the toilet stall
I lean easy, musing
on the dear small sounds of you

a moment later, hear the crack,
a sharp report through paper.
The cup. My breath fails.
Under the door your red hands
reach for the sack. It
swings sad between your feet,
clinking like a bag of nails.

You emerge, your face
suffused with effort of
resisting private tears
in this public place.

I recall the grace of your hands,
seabirds flirting in caves
my morning estuaries, ruddy
with the taste of salt and sand

remember too
however she may love
a carpenter lives
by her hands,

and find my gift of language silenced
rudely by your pain.

What speech, what spells
what revolution
can make this moment whole again?

Nancy Mairs ————————————————

Shape

I am listening to *The Doors' Greatest Hits*. It is Abby's album. She bought it last week, along with something called *Scary Monsters/Super Creeps* by David Bowie, and I was amused that she would spend her carefully hoarded babysitting money on the songs that she heard while she was cutting her teeth and tottering from couch to coffee table to chair and riding on her father's shoulders in peace marches on the commons of all the towns around Boston. But The Doors are popular again, as are The Beatles and Jimi Hendrix and even Cream. These children seem nostalgic for a life they never lived—for *my* life—and I find their nostalgia odd and touching, a kind of statement about the charmed existence I must have had, though I was not much aware of the charm at the time.

Under my fingers a head is taking shape. The afternoon is hot, and the clay against my palms feels as warm as flesh. For several weeks now I have felt heavy, doughy, especially in my head, and my vision has been blurred. But this morning, in spite of the thunderous August heat, I woke to lightness and clarity. That's the part of having multiple sclerosis I find hardest to deal with—the unpredictability with which the symptoms come and go. I just get used to living one way when I shift to another. Today, at last, I felt like working, and I have been at it for a couple of hours now. The head is strange, elongated, with high cheekbones and a pointed chin and protuberant eyes, embryonic somehow, like the head of a six-month fetus in one of those photos by Nilssen. It doesn't look like my usual work at all. I seldom do any part of the human form. I do animals—cats, mostly. There's a good demand for them, and although Michael is generous with what he has, it never seems to be enough, especially now that David is in college. So I can use the money.

Over the music I hear the telephone ring and then stop ringing. Since it is Saturday, the call will be for Abby, and I am glad I don't have to stop working to answer it. The ringing pushes me back past The Doors, past confused images of newly baked potato bread and "We Shall Overcome" and diapers frozen to the clothesline, of friends drinking Burgundy and writing slogans in Magic Marker on white posterboard in the kitchen of the bare white apartment outside Porter Square, back to a much earlier period, when I was just about Abby's age and had fallen in love for the first time. With Allen, a tall skinny boy, red-headed and freckled, who was in love not with me but with World War II battleships and planes. Abby loves me to tell her about Allen, and I charm her sometimes with the story of how I had to battle the battleships and planes, and how every day on the bus ride to and from school I did, though I don't remember now precisely what weapons were in my arsenal, until finally, not long before the prom, I could feel myself coming into focus in Allen's sights. Then began the battle of nerves, as every night I sat at my desk working algebra problems or reading *Romeo and Juliet* while I waited for the telephone, which I pretended not to hear, and for my mother's voice calling, "Pamela, telephone!"

Allen never did call, but later others did, and I have never quite shaken the slight catch of breath at the ringing of the telephone, which seldom rings anymore for me. Sometimes it does, of course. There are still food-service plans and insurance salespeople in the world and, more important, gallery owners and a few friends, but some of those drifted away when I first got sick, and more when Michael and I got divorced, and the others leave the city every weekend in the summer, For a moment I wish that I still had a lover, that Jeremy would come back, just so I'd have some reason to listen for the telephone. My life, scrubbed of romantic possibilities, is serene, open, but assuredly flat. Come winter I'll get more calls, I think, and then I'll pull out of this funk into which heat and humidity, acting on a whimsical nervous system, have thrown me. I'll probably even start feeling harrassed.

I feel good about the head, which is emerging more and more clearly from the damp brownish clay. One of my friends in the art department at Brandeis has been after me to teach a sculpture course, but I have thought that two trips a week would be too tiring. Looking at the head, I decide to call him on Monday and say that I'll try it for a semester.

Abby comes into my studio and I twist around to look at her. She is wearing a red towel around her body and a purple one around her head. She is a lovely color, almost like that of my clay, since she has been working every weekday morning this summer as a mother's helper, taking a neighbor's children to a nearby park. She hates the children, who have been raised to treat anyone over four feet tall as a serf, but she likes the money. She is saving for a trip to San Francisco to see her friend Samuel, whose father has just transferred to the zoo there because it has better snakes. Red and purple and brown, she looks sumptuous, like an Aztec princess, and I think, not for the first time, that one of the many things Michael gave me was two exotic children, grafted like mangoes onto the apple stem of my Yankee family.

"Hi, Abby," I say, looking back down at my hands. "Who was on the phone?"

"Harriet. She's back from Nova Scotia." Her voice, raised above the music, sounds high and clear, as though she is shouting from a great distance.

"Did she have a good time?"

"Yeah, so-so, I guess. Can you take us to the movies tonight? We want to see *The Stunt Man.*"

"Oh Lord, Abby," I sigh. I want to see *The Stunt Man* too, and she knows it, but I don't want to see it tonight. My left wrist is getting floppy and the small of my back, where the muscles are weakest, feels tight and sore from being upright for several hours. I want to take a cool bath and make a fruit salad for supper and spend the evening lying in front of the television. "Can't you take the bus?"

"Wouldn't do any good. The movie's rated R."

"Oh damn, of course it is. How about Harriet's father—could he take you?" Harriet's mother died of cancer a couple of years ago, and I feel guilty about suggesting her father, since he transports the girls too often as it is, but maybe he wouldn't mind just once more.

"Harriet's father has gone to New York. She's staying with her grandmother, *who doesn't have a license,*" she finishes in a rush, anticipating me.

"I'm sorry, Abby, but not tonight. I've been working very hard this afternoon, and I'm just too tired to go out."

"But we could go to the early show."

"Maybe tomorrow night."

"Je-*sus,* Mother." She snatches the red towel, which has begun to undrape itself. "No wonder Father left you." Her head is down as she tucks the end of the towel between her breasts, but she speaks distinctly. "Harriet's right—you're nothing but a damned cripple."

"Riders on the Storm" ends, and the record clicks off. In the sudden silence I can hear Abby's breath against the back of her right hand; above the palm her eyes are wide. Still clutching the towel in her left hand, she turns and runs out of the studio, kicking the door shut behind her.

The quiet in the room seems creepy. I wipe most of the clay off my hands with a damp rag and then push the swivel chair I work in over to the stereo and turn the record over. My hands have started trembling, as they always do now when I get upset. I have a hard time getting The Doors going again.

What Abby has said seems to be inevitable. I shouldn't feel so shocked. The only real surprise is that it took her so long. After all, we've been living alone together for nearly a year, ever since David left for Emory, longer really, since David's independence kept him out of the house as much as in. But at least he sometimes took Abby with him, skating or sailing or hiking the Appalachian Trail, and she didn't have to depend on me so much for companionship and transportation. At the beginning of the summer I was relieved when their father offered to fly them both down to spend their vacation with him, that although David accepted, Abby refused, wanting to spend the last bit of time she could with Samuel. I didn't want to face the uncertainty of a summer alone. But maybe she should have gone.

Abby is wrong, of course, about why Michael left me, but I can't think how to tell her that. I don't understand his reasons entirely myself. He never liked explanations. I only know that he began to leave quite a while ago, before he knew there was anything wrong with me, before I was really aware of it myself. His leaving seemed not to have very much at all to do with me personally, in fact. I think that he liked me that he still likes me. From a distance. Perhaps he was homesick. I don't know. For a while I thought there might be another woman, after a female voice called and asked for "Miguel," but when I told him about the call, he said it was a secretary from the consulate answering a question he had had about his visa, and I suspect that he was telling the truth.

"I'm going to go home," he told me one afternoon, coming into the studio with a sheaf of the yellow onionskin on which his sister wrote to him, with neat angular black strokes, every week. "My mother is getting worse."

I was still working in wood then, and I had been experimenting with a crude whittled effect, using the big blade of the Swiss Army knife David had given me for Christmas. The blade had slipped and bitten into the first knuckle of my left forefinger, and now I was sitting in front of the chunk of pale wood with an ice cube wrapped in paper towel against the cut. Michael looked at my hands, then went out to the bathroom and came back with scissors, Dermaplast, gauze pads, adhesive tape. He pulled the wet pinkish paper towel away and sprayed the cut.

"Does it hurt?" he asked, wrapping the finger in gauze.

"No, not much."

"I don't think it's too deep." He cut off some strips of tape and wound them loosely around the padded finger.

"Shall I come with you?" I asked. I knew the answer, but the habit of courtesy between us dictated the question.

"No, I think not," he said. "But thank you for offering." He kissed the finger, as we had always done when patching up Abby or David or one another, and went back out.

Not long afterward I cut myself again, that time on the back of my hand, and I realized that I was getting too clumsy to handle the tools safety, so I gave up wood, though I still think about it, the grain and weight and fragrance.

Once Michael decided to go, he went quickly, quitting his job with the Boston Industrial Mission, settling his affairs with me, and flying out in just over two weeks. I missed him, I still miss him sometimes, but I get as much from his long, meticulous letters as I did from living with him toward the end, maybe more. How can I explain this amiable dissolution of the marriage bond to my passionate fifteen-year-old daughter?

Easier, perhaps, to explain to her about Jeremy, for if anyone was troubled by my being a damned cripple, it was Jeremy, not Michael. I don't think about Jeremy very often anymore, and I am surprised to be thinking of him again today. Earlier I was remembering how he told me about losing his virginity to a psychology graduate student while "Light My Fire" played over and over on the stereo. He brought the whole clumsy, strained procedure to life in a few sentences, between sips of beer, and I laughed, watching his eyes, his heavy mouth, trying to reconstruct the eighteen-year-old in this aging boy with whom I was falling in love.

I met Jeremy a year ago last spring, not long after Michael left, when he moved to the city and started walking his dog along the river, where I walked my dog; and we had an affair that ended as abruptly as it began. It began with the dogs, of course. Mine was a small mongrel named Thoby Stephen, black with white chest and forepaws and a terrier-style moustache going grey; his was something large and white and purebred which I can still see clearly but whose name I seem to have forgotten. They found one another on a smoky day in late April in the middle of a plot of red and yellow tulips, in which they rolled and snarled and snapped until Jeremy, wading in among the flattened stems and broken petals, hauled Thoby out and shoved him at me, muttering something about keeping my god-damned dog on a leash. His dog was off the leash too, but it seemed egregious to point that out. I snapped Thoby onto the chain; Jeremy leashed his dog; and the two entered a pact of neutrality that permitted Jeremy and me to walk side by side.

Before long we found ourselves hurrying to the river every afternoon, and soon Jeremy asked me to his place for tea, but it turned out that my place was closer, so we went there. Thoby, however, although he had learned to tolerate Jeremy's dog in a public place, could not bear him in his own territory, and tea turned out to be an awkward affair, punctuated by growls and the baring of teeth. After that, Jeremy and I left the dogs home when we visited one another. We still walked them together frequently, though, and when at the end of the summer I had an attack while Abby and David were camping in the Berkshires, and could take only a few steps at a time, Jeremy came for Thoby twice a day.

But as soon as the children came back, he told me he no longer wanted to sleep with me. That's what he said, sitting on the top step of my front porch pulling a thorn out of one of Thoby's pads with a pair of tweezers: "I no longer want to sleep with you." He dropped the thorn over the railing. Thoby licked Jeremy's cheek once, then settled down to work on the injured paw.

"Why?" I asked, and felt like a fool. I got what I asked for: Jeremy needed more space in which to be himself, more time to work on his dissertation, more freedom to be with other women if he felt like it. I think he honestly couldn't imagine that a woman could want to live without a man, especially a woman who was likely to be struck helpless at any moment. My man had left me, so I must be looking for another. He looked at my blunt fingers as though they were claws. Perhaps he could actually feel them sink into the flesh of his shoulders. Perhaps he was imagining what it would be like to wake up one morning next to a woman blind, dumb, limbs twitching, bathed in her own urine. I wouldn't blame him. My future is not one to be taken lightly. I was still too weak then to walk Thoby, so when Abby and David went back to school, I gave him to some friends who have an acre of land around their house in Sudbury, and he died not long after. He was an old dog.

When I started going out again, I ran into Jeremy a few times, and he always said something about our still being friends and how we must get together sometime to talk, and I said each time, "Fine. You call me." But he didn't, and after a while I ran into a woman at a watercolor show who knew Jeremy and thought he had moved away, somewhere in the South, Alabama, maybe. Since then I have thought of Jeremy off and on, floating through the rank green Alabama countryside in his space like a bubble, his palms and nose pressed to the transparent curve, and I have wondered if he wasn't, in some way, challenging me to break the bubble. If so, he was challenging the wrong person. After twenty years of marriage, I grant space as automatically as the Cambridge Savings Bank pays me five-and-a-quarter on my account. Which is not to say that I don't miss Jeremy. I do. And he probably wasn't challenging me anyway. He looked just as happy the last time he walked down the steps, past the day lilies, out into the street, as he ever had.

Some of this I could probably explain to Abby, but I don't want to.

I have been looking at the long blind elegant head in front of me without touching it. The Doors have howled their way through "L.A. Woman" and stopped; the room is once again quiet. I will not do any more work today. Anyway, the head, rough as it is, seems almost finished. I swaddle it in a plastic Rainbo bread bag like an amniotic sac through which it stares blindly at me in the last light of the August afternoon.

Maybe I should take Abby and Harriet to the movies. But I think of throwing together some dinner and putting on my brace and getting into the car and driving to the theater and sitting through the movie and driving home again. I am tired. I am also afraid, I realize. I am afraid of losing Abby. I am afraid that if I refuse to take her to the movies, she will leave me. She will decide to go live with her father, and then I will be alone. Michael has gone, and David, and Thoby, and Jeremy, and if Abby goes there will be no one in the house but me and the spooky striped cat Abby brought me from the Humane Society after I had to give Thoby away. I will become a cartoon character—Old Woman with Pussycat—something straight out of George Booth. I don't even know if I can keep the silly beast in fresh food and kitty litter.

I am afraid, and the room is getting dark. I can hardly see through the dusk. I have been picking the clay from under my fingernails, but my hands still feel puckered and gritty. If I take Abby and Harriet to the movies, then tomorrow I may be too tired to work. I have been thinking about hands, a torso, Michael's high tight buttocks the first time I ever saw them, pale as stone in the half-light of a rainy late-winter afternoon.

I fish my cane from under the chair and get up. Because I am still shaky, I grope my way to Abby's room with one hand against the wall, feeling like a cripple. The door is open. In some indefinable way, the room seems feminine, in spite of David's old Star Trek bedspreads and his Sierra Club posters all over the walls. Maybe it's just Abby herself, sitting cross-legged on the bed nearest the window. She has shed the towels and is wearing cut-offs and a Bruce Springsteen T-shirt. Her dark hair, parted in the middle, falls straight and damp almost to her waist. Crying has lengthened and thinned her face. Her eyes seem too large. If she goes to her father I will be very lonely.

"Abby," I say, "come." I take her hand, and it lies against my palm as limp and hot as it used to when I walked her to nursery school. "Come and see the funny head I've just done."

Vassar Miller ————————————————————

Faux Pas

I sat with you in a back pew when
your father died; for you, stared at so long,
would not gape at the helpless dead.

At your mother's funeral I thought to sit
in the same place beside you, decent as always
to the point of fault. Who would have guessed!

Dear friend, forgive my unaverted eyes.
But there's no back row of the mind to hide
here from the horror of your dying.

A Woman Dead in Her Forties

1.
Your breasts/   sliced-off   The scars
dimmed   as they would have to be
years later

All the women I grew up with are sitting
half-naked on rocks   in sun
we look at each other and
are not ashamed

and you too have taken off your blouse
but this was not what you wanted:

to show your scarred, deleted torso

I barely glance at you
as if my look could scald you
though I'm the one who loved you

I want to touch my fingers
to where your breasts had been
but we never did such things

You hadn't thought everyone
would look so perfect
unmutilated

you pull on
your blouse again: stern statement:

There are things I will not share
with everyone

2.
You send me back to share
my own scars   first of all
with myself

What did I hide from her
what have I denied her
what losses suffered

how in this ignorant body
did she hide

waiting for her release
till uncontrollable light began to pour

from every wound and suture
and all the sacred openings

3.
Wartime.   We sit on warm
weathered, softening grey boards

the ladder glimmers where you told me
the leeches swim

I smell the flame
of kerosene   the pine

boards where we sleep side by side
in narrow cots

the night-meadow exhaling
its darkness   calling

child into woman
child into woman
woman

4.
Most of our love from the age of nine
took the form of jokes and mute

loyalty: you fought a girl
who said she'd knock me down

we did each other's homework
wrote letters   kept in touch, untouching

lied about our lives: I wearing
the face of the proper marriage

you the face of the independent woman
We cleaved to each other across that space

fingering webs
of love and estrangement   till the day

the gynecologist touched your breast
and found a palpable hardness

5.
You played heroic, necessary
games with death

since in your neo-protestant tribe the void
was supposed not to exist

except as a fashionable concept
you had no traffic with

I wish you were here tonight   I want
to yell at you

Don't accept
Don't give in

But would I be meaning your brave
irreproachable life, you dean of women, or

your unfair, unfashionable, unforgivable
woman's death?

6.
You are every woman I ever loved
and disavowed

a bloody incandescent chord strung out
across years, tracts of space

How can I reconcile this passion
with our modesty

your calvinist heritage
my girlhood frozen into forms

how can I go on this mission
without you

you, who might have told me
everything you feel is true?

7.
Time after time in dreams you rise
reproachful

once from a wheelchair pushed by your father
across a lethal expressway

Of all my dead it's you
who come to me unfinished

You left me amber beads
strung with turquoise from an Egyptian grave

I wear them wondering
How am I true to you?

I'm half-afraid to write poetry
for you   who never read it much

and I'm left laboring
with the secrets and the silence

In plain language: I never told you how I loved you
we never talked at your deathbed of your death

8.
One autumn evening in a train
catching the diamond-flash of sunset

in puddles along the Hudson
I thought: *I understand*

life and death now, the choices
I didn't know your choice

or how by then you had no choice
how the body tells the truth in its rush of cells

Most of our love took the form
of mute loyalty

we never spoke at your deathbed of your death

but from here on
I want more crazy mourning, more howl, more keening

We stayed mute and disloyal
because we were afraid

I would have touched my fingers
to where your breasts had been
but we never did such things

Part III

Transcendence

Many of the works in Parts 1 and 2 of this book deal with overcoming attitudinal and societal barriers in our everyday lives, our relationships, our workplaces. The selections in Part 3 deal with overcoming different kinds of barriers: the barriers inside ourselves. One of the most insidious aspects of oppression is that, being targets of incorrect assumptions, stereotyped notions, and invalidating messages about who we are, sometimes even from our closest family and beloved friends, we begin to believe they are true; we internalize the oppression. Our barriers become self-imposed; now our challenge is to transcend these internal limits, to experience our own strengths, perceive our true beauty, know our real value.

Help in transcending our barriers does come sometimes from the outside. In "Mendings," Muriel Rukeyser pays homage to a healer who offered her a fresh and deeply human perspective on illness. Such a perspective is rare. More commonly we encounter eager helpers with motives that arise from their own confusion and their own deep needs; thus their interventions are not only unhelpful but actually interfere. In Mary E. Wilkins Freeman's 1887 story "A Mistaken Charity," two elder women, one deaf and one blind, foil their helpers' misguided efforts to put them in a geriatric home, and demonstrate their success in interdependence. Like many other writers since her time, Freeman attempts to dispel the myth that disabled people are completely dependent upon the help of others, incapable of taking the lead. In "The Body's Memory," Jean Stewart asserts her essential need, in seeking to transcend her own fear, to live alone, despite the puzzlement of well-meaning friends.

Disabled women are typically regarded by the culture at two extremes: on the one hand, our lives are thought to be pitiful, full of pain, the result of senseless tragedy; on the other hand, we are seen as inspirational beings, nearly raised to sainthood by those who perceive our suffering with awe. Vassar Miller, in her poem "Posthumous Letter to Thomas Merton," writes, "Do not we sufferers always inhabit/ The edges of the world as pioneers/ To prove how much humanity can bear/ And still be human?" *(If I Could Sleep Deeply Enough,* Liveright, 1974). What is the value of our struggle? Is it worth it? Each woman must decide for herself.

We seek meaning in our experience. Many women turn to or develop a spiritual or religious perspective in hope of attaining a sense that their lives are part of a grand schema, a larger plan that validates, indeed, necessitates their particular body and life. Laurel Lee, in *Walking through the Fire* finds solace and guidance from God, support and hope from her church. What is this hope? A belief in the possibility of change, a force that keeps us going in the most difficult of times. In "Days of Recovery," Carole Stone finds hope and renewal in the act of writing. Deborah Kendrick celebrates the triumph of hope in "20/20 with a Twist," a futuristic story in which the environment is completely altered to serve the needs of blind people. Hope, however, is not denial of reality. Nancy Mairs, while exploring the profound and valuable lessons of disability in her essay, "On Being a Cripple," states emphatically: "If a cure were found, would I take it? In a minute."

With the presence of hope, we can make a distinction between the pain, the struggle of the moment, and the clarity we can achieve with time and thought. Nancy Mairs may cry out "I'm so sick of being a cripple!" But she then proceeds to reflect that the disability itself is distinct from her distress about it; she has a choice in how she regards herself, her disease, her lifestyle.

We are not bound by traditional definitions of what it means to be disabled. The more insight we gain, the more we realize that nearly *everything* the culture has told us about the experience of disability and illness (the burden, the tragedy, the suffering, the limits) is based on arbitrary sets of values. There is no evidence that our experiences are universally negative or bad. In other cultures, some native American, for example, people with disabilities are regarded as spiritually special and are assigned healing powers and leadership roles.

All of the works in this part in some way attest to the possibility that we can free ourselves of cultural notions about disability and illness. Muriel Rukeyser, in "St. Roach," looks freshly at the world and at beings for what they are, not as they have been commonly defined. And in "The Wards," she shows that illness can offer startling insights into human experience: "Our selves lit clear,/ . . . we risk everything,/ Walking into life." Adrienne Rich, in "Transit," wonders whether it is the "skier" or the "cripple" who is most haunted by the reflection of the other as they pass at the foot of the mountain. In her essay "Beauty: When the Other Dancer Is the Self," Alice Walker shows how her three-year-old daughter's untarnished perspective helps her reverse years of self-invalidation.

A friend who uses an electric wheelchair because of generalized muscle weakness sports a t-shirt that exhorts "Fight Gravity." Mobility, with such a condition, would not be limited if one lived on the moon or some other environ with reduced gravity. Ironically, the t-shirt is made by a hiking club; here we find rock climbers and quadriplegics with a common opponent. We also find that disability can be regarded as a function of the environment, not merely of one's body limitations.

In her recent book *Everyone Here Spoke Sign Language* (Harvard University Press, 1985), Nora E. Groce tells the story of the largely deaf population of Martha's Vineyard, an island off the coast of Massachusetts, during the seventeenth and eighteenth centuries. Because the gene pool was so isolated, the trait for deafness appeared often in each generation. With deafness being so common, the community adapted. Everyone learned sign language, and the stigma of limitation attached to deafness disappeared from the culture. In marked contrast to the debilitating oppression the deaf community now experiences in the general culture, deaf people on Martha's Vineyard were landowners, politicians, respected citizens. In the context of a favorable environment, disability becomes a benign characteristic, a unique but innocuous aspect of one's being. Jean Stewart takes us to such a new environment in her poem "What the Fish Feels." Here we see that disability does not detract from our essential being. No matter how uniquely our physical being presents us, we are women, we are human, we are truly and fully alive.

from Walking through the Fire: A Hospital Journal

Biopsy Day
Friday, May 21, 1976

It wasn't an early priority surgery, but it was to be done before noon. I decided the lymph enlargements were guilty of disease and had to be proven innocent. In this attitude I could have no letdown from pathology. Only the pubic hair on the right side was removed, and I was given enough medication so that I would be relaxed during the incision procedure.

The first effect of the narcotic was that I began staring at a quilt that I had mounted at the foot of the bed, becoming wrapped in its design and color. . . .

I was wheeled into surgery and transferred to the table. I was draped except for my face and entire groin area. Above Dr. Temple were two large lights that seemed like large bug's eyes, but not of a menacing species.

In this X-rated position, the staff surgeon walked in, looked at me, and asked Dr. Temple which side the biopsy was to be performed on.

Our minds can bring forth data in less than a second. I was immediately reminded of my first biopsy, when all the betadine preps were done on the left of my neck and without comment the node was removed from the right.

So I sat up on the table, looked at the staff surgeon and said, "The side where they shaved."

Then it was obvious that it was a dumb question. The nurses and doctors looked each other in the eyes, but the surgeon's position prevented us from laughing. It was one of those little moments common to all, where the emperor in the parade discovers he has no clothes on. We were the only two that had spoken, and without another word he left the operating room.

Dr. Temple made the incision. I could feel the blood run down my thigh.

Mike Mainer once shared in detail how a cesarean section is performed. I remembered all the steps and began to abstract. I allowed free play in my ideas and decided I was having a minute cesarean and was going to give birth to an infant the size of my thumbnail. I slept the rest of the afternoon.

A hematologist examined me. He had a closet of pet lions, and his recommendations unleashed several for my contemplation. Their mouths were open.

"Although she is still, clinically, in Stage III, the severity of the symptoms makes more widespread involvement a possibility. Because of this, chemotherapy (MOP) is in order. Normally, patient would be rested four to six weeks, completing radiation. However, because of the aggressiveness of the disease in this patient, that time may not be available. We are waiting staff's opinion as to this.

"Suggest:
1. gallium scan
2. bone marrow
3. bone scan
4. liver scan
5. liver function test
6. surgical consultant for biopsy of inguinal mass"

These lions stayed in my room. At times they were very big, and I would tremble. Sometimes they were small, but they were always present, with teeth.

The biopsy report confirmed the spread of Hodgkin's. There were days to wait before Dr. Bagby and the staff returned from their convention. It was a time for me to consider the possibility of chemotherapy.

Dr. Ritzman sent a friend of his with fourth-stage Hodgkin's to my room. He said the only reason he was alive was chemotherapy.

But once Dr. Hood had said, "I've killed people with chemotherapy."

One text wrote, "Significantly, the sites of major toxicity of these chemotherapeutic agents are not all the same: Although most are myelotoxic, some primarily affect the nervous system or gastrointestinal tract" (*Cancer Journal for Clinicians,* December 1975).

Besides the concern of the cancer-causing agents, I did not want the top of my head to look like my knee. A disease and its treatment can be a series of humiliations, a chisel for humility.

My room had been an ice-skating rink. As I sat and wrote, I glided through the hours, leaped over barrels, and was exuberant.

Now there were holes I had to maneuver around. My feet could get wet and cold, and I would shiver on the bed.

I had an official pass for a weekend afternoon. I asked Richard if we could take a ride in the country. I was starved for landscape. I got dressed but he never came.

I felt like a sociology documentary I once saw of the unwed mother. Often she vests her expectations of security in a boyfriend who never comes to see her in the unwed mothers' home.

Later I reached him by telephone and he said he had taken Matthew, Anna, and some other children hiking.

The same weekend Mike Mainer asked me if I would like to go for a ride with him.

I asked Richard and he said it was a good idea. Mike had a small German car with a window in the roof. We drove west through sloping farm fields. One meadow had a track of red flowers like a solid letter spelled into the earth.

"It's clover," I said.

"It's not clover," said Mike.

He backed up the car to settle the horticultural question. It was a crimson clover variety.

We waded out and I lay down in the scarlet verdure. It reminded me of when I was a child in Illinois and we would make imprints of angels in the fresh snow. We would wave our arms and legs into wings and dresses.

"Mike, there really is a Heaven," I said.

"I can't believe that," he answered.

"If we stood back in history three hundred years and I brought you a report of a continent I found with animals so different from those on your farm, you wouldn't have believed me then, either."

We ate tacos in a drive-in. We went back to the hospital. I shared with him one square of my worry about Richard's attitude toward me.

"Stay as close to him as you can," Mike told me.

Friends arranged to bring my children for a few hours. I was so excited. I went up to the pediatric floor and walked past the wall mural of Snow White into the game room. I explained to the volunteer that I wanted to borrow some toys and I would bring them back. I filled a red wagon with mechanical wonders, stories, and dolls. I took the stars and left the cast of thousands.

I got a bowl of crushed ice and little bags of a crunchy kind of food.

The children came; ever moving, ever talking bursts of energy. They had a style of appearing to explode into an infinity of perceiving parts. We flowed together.

When they left I was so exhausted I could hardly move or speak. I wanted to remove the toys. A sadness permeated my being. Maybe all the storybooks had sad endings. I hit the wrong floor button and wandered around, a stranger pulling a crazy wagon in her nightgown.

As I slept a nurse took the cloth wrapping off a sterile instrument. He smoothed out the material. He painted with a blue flow pen a moon face with wide eyes and an enormous crescent smile.

He climbed over my bed. He climbed over my plants and hung this banner down from my window, using the extra-wide masking tape.

It was the first thing I saw in the morning.

———

The day came when some of the hematologist's six recommended points would stick me. They were planning to do a bone marrow. I waited.

The hematology staff chief had returned; he came into my room with Dr. Bagby and Mike Mainer. He said he was not convinced that chemotherapy or any of the tests were at all necessary. The inguinal nodes were an untreated radiation port, thus their enlargement did not mean I had had a relapse. His recommendation was a discharge from the hospital, with a further course of radiation on an outpatient basis.

He took every lion with him. I roared for joy. I wanted to tear up that first hematologist. As Mike Mainer left the room, he told me to "Love thy neighbor as thyself," and closed the door.

On my very last day, a man came and introduced himself as the technician who once gave me a barium swallow. "Look," he said, "these are the stains on my pants when you spit out the drink."

I took down the quilts, put the plants back and went home.

Thursday, May 27

Home is said to be the one place you can go and they have to take you in. If I'm a rock thrown in the water, home is one of the first rings from the weight. It is you in things.

I walked into someone else's house at my old-shoe address.

The living room was not the grandmother lace card where I once read *David Copperfield*. Now there was a television set against the wall.

I had only allowed the kitchen counter a line of antique cans. Now there was a beach of practical kitchen movement: A silver toaster has its electric-cord hand under a blender umbrella; an electric can opener was wearing a green plastic bikini; tacky vendor stands of canisters advertised "flour" and "sugar."

"This is how it's going to stay. I couldn't find anything," said Richard. "And that stove," indicating my blue enamel queen on her ornate throne, "has to go. It makes the pans black."

So I walked through the house and the floors were slanted uphill.

Friday, May 28

Richard took the children to the baby-sitter.

Saturday

He helped the baby-sitter take her dirty clothes to the laundromat. She was a young girl raising two children alone and her car didn't work.

Sunday

There was the day my house fell down.
Remember it brown,
Like the ground.

I always operated under ordinances. I was allowed Sunday school and that was my formal religious training time boundary. The children went to their classes and I sat in the back, listening to adult admonitions.

The pastor's wife asked if I would stay and share from the pulpit in the main service. It was like a new application of working out my salvation with fear and trembling. An elder escorted me to the platform after the congregation sang:

Storm clouds will come
Strong winds will blow,
But I've got a Savior
And He's sweet I know.

The faces spread out before me. There was a television camera for the auxiliary room. It's a large congregation.

I made paragraphs. I left the rostrum. I left my Bible. I left the church. I was tired.

Richard took the children hiking. It was raining and they were wrapped in blue nylon zip suits. His last words were, "The fire will go out in three hours."

The pastor's wife came by with my old ragged-flag Bible. She brought me a new one with large print and references. The elders had signed it. I paraphrased their message to "keep on trucking."

Richard never came home. It was night. *If I were a mouse in a cold old house, what a cold old mouse I would be.*

I called the baby-sitter. They were there. They had all gone hiking together.

Thoughts flew around in my head. I understood that to him I was dead.

We talked that night. "We're in two different kingdoms." he said.

How can two walk together unless they be agreed? The feeling of love that promotes tap-dancing down supermarket aisles, leaping over bushes, catching blooms between the toes; that goes. But the fact of love becomes a code of behavior.

"Love suffers long, and is kind, seeks not its own, is not easily provoked." But there is only rest when every eye stays in the nest.

As I put the children to bed late that night, they leaned out of their bunks built from plate glass packing crates to sing. They had Sunday school songs. They pounded their fists one on top of the other and the lyrics ran:

The wise man built his house upon the rock
And the house on the rock stood firm.

The storm came up,
And the rain came down,
And the house on the rock stood firm.
The foolish man built his house upon the sand
The storm came up,
And the rain came down
And the house on the sand went squish . . .

They spread out their fingers and sang it again.

Monday, Memorial Day

Friends opened houses to me. Richard started to file for divorce.

The Wade family was a cloud of dew in my summer heat. I had my radiation series to slug out and I slid each night into their home plate. They gave me their bed, and they slept on the couch. The Wades had two little girls. I watched the family well and long; they were sound.

I ached in concern for my children. They came to visit me. It was a comfort that youth could be so insulated by their merry hearts.

I was in the wilderness of my life. I was a Gretel without a Hansel lost in the woods. There was a wicked witch who would eat me if I would listen. *In my thoughts were my wars fought.*

Weeping may endure for the night,
But joy cometh in the morning (Psalms 30:5).

I rented the upstairs of an old house. I turned each window into a greenhouse. The children came home. Anna played Maple Leaf, a child's interpretation of the words *make believe.* There was no more outbreak of Hodgkin's disease among the doll family. The dolls only had colds.

I finished my journal. I was shy to show it, but I gave it to Mike Mainer. From him it passed in and out of the residents' mailboxes.

I had my last radiation treatment. I was young again. I had completed all the medical course possible unless the disease recurred.

In Oregon, the salmon run from the sea to their spawning ground. There are nets. There are sporting men. There are rocks and ascents so steep some die from the journey itself. But some silver salmon make it home. It's a matter of percentage; it always is. I could grow old.

My last treatment was the very day family practice clinic had a farewell dinner for its graduating residents. We ate on the roof in the sunshine.

Stu could only grab a hasty plate, as he still had tables up and down the hall to serve, like a Dr. Waiter.

I pretended that I was graduating, too.

The head of family practice put his arms straight out to the side and said, "I'm an airplane."

"I'm a cloud," I said, and he hugged me.

I met another guest in the hall, Stu's sage, Dr. Mack Lipkin from New York.

After that day Stu called and organized a videotape session with Mack Lipkin and myself.

Dr. Lipkin came into the studio reading my book. He had his thumb on the page where the breast pump looked like a bicycle horn.

Stu cared more about our comfort than the clarity of the recorded picture. He dimmed the major illuminating lamps to reduce the heat.

I had borrowed a copy of Mack Lipkin's book. He's an authority in his field, and has served as a consultant to the Surgeon General. I shared one of my favorite paragraphs, where Dr. Lipkin was speaking with the head of a major medical center. He told him that he thinks it should be required that every graduating doctor first produce a bowel movement in a horizontal position with three witnesses present.

"Is that right?" asked Stu.

"Yes," said Dr. Lipkin.

Dr. Lipkin asked me to come to his office the following Monday at nine in the morning.

After an eclipse, the sun emerges from the shadow.

One morning a man from church came to my door and offered me a scholarship to Bible school.

Friends contributed to buy me a round-trip airplane ticket. It was a vacation in a box addressed "to Mexico for Laurel." The children were to go to their grandparents' house while I traveled south.

Monday, July 26, 1976

I had to hurry to make my appointment. I rushed out into the early morning street and waited for my bus.

An antique store had been closed for a long time. This was the day they were loading the furniture onto a large rented truck.

"Oh," I sighed, knowing I should wait for the bus, but I entered the shop. The owner sold me a wooden cuckoo clock for a quarter. I turned its face into my dress so it looked like I was only carrying a large birdhouse.

The owner went and stood on the curb, overseeing the hoisting of his furniture pieces.

I saw the orange bus at the top of the hill, "Look, I didn't miss it at all."

The proprietor emerged again and gave a gift to me. It was a rich leather book called *Blessed Be God*. The pictures were in such hairline detail they could be printed into religious paper money.

I entered Dr. Lipkin's office on the third floor of the family practice building.

He said he found some charm in my book and asked to send it to an editor friend in New York.

I felt like I was a very homely girl who someone thought could be in a beauty contest.

I jumped up and down in my chair and somehow this activated the clock in my lap. It went "Cuckoo, cuckoo" over and over until I thought I was flying over the cuckoo's nest.

What could I give Mack Lipkin, wise sage, great doctor? I had a little sketchbook of watercolors I had made of passages in Thoreau's *Walden*. I ripped out a favorite page: "The essential laws of man's existence do not change just as our bones are indistinguishable from those of our ancestors."

My book went to New York. It was like a piece of paper a child floats out into a stream. It was soon out of sight. It will get caught in some weeds, I thought. There are holes in it. It will fill with water and sink.

But I lifted up and flew on.

Muriel Rukeyser —————————————————————————

St. Roach

For that I never knew you, I only learned to dread you,
for that I never touched you, they told me you are filth,
they showed me by every action to despise your kind;
for that I saw my people making war on you,
I could not tell you apart, one from another,
for that in childhood I lived in places clear of you,
for that all the people I knew met you by
crushing you, stamping you to death, they poured boiling
    water on you, they flushed you down,
for that I could not tell one from another
only that you were dark, fast on your feet, and slender.
    Not like me.
For that I did not know your poems
And that I do not know any of your sayings
And that I cannot speak or read your language
And that I do not sing your songs

And that I do not teach our children
to eat your food
or know your poems
or sing your songs
But that we say you are filthing our food
But that we know you not at all.

Yesterday I looked at one of you for the first time.
You were lighter than the others in color, that was
neither good nor bad.

Mendings

You made healing as you wanted us to make bread and poems.
In your abrasive life of gifts,
In the little ravine telling the life of the future
When your science would be given to all,
A broken smile,
In the sun, speaking of the joining of nerve-endings,
Make the wounds part of the well body.
Make a healed life.
You shouted, waving your hand with the last phalange
Of the little finger missing, you whole man,
"Make it well! Make things accessible!"
He is a pollinating man. We are his seedlings.
Marshak, I was your broken nerve-endings,
You made your man-made bridges over the broken nerves.
What did you do? Inspect potatoes, wait for passports, do your research,
While the State Department lady was saying, "Let him swim,"
While the chief who had the power to allow your uses
To move, a proper use of plastic, a bridge across broken nerves
Stopped you there (and asked me to marry him).
Saying to you, Marshak, full of creation as the time
Went deeper into war, and you to death:
"The war will be over before your work is ready."

Nancy Mairs

On Being a Cripple

To escape is nothing. Not to escape is nothing.
                                        —Louise Bogan

The other day I was thinking of writing an essay on being a cripple. I was thinking hard in one of the stalls of the women's room in my office building, as I was shoving my shirt into my jeans and tugging up my zipper. Preoccupied, I flushed, picked up my book bag, took my cane down from the hook, and unlatched the door. So many movements unbalanced me, and as I pulled the door open I fell over backward, landing fully clothed on the toilet seat with my legs splayed in front of me: the old beetle-on-its-back routine. Saturday afternoon, the building deserted, I was free to laugh aloud as I wriggled back to my feet, my voice bouncing off the yellowish tiles from all directions. Had anyone been there with me, I'd have been still and faint and hot with chagrin.

I decided that it was high time to write the essay.

First, the matter of semantics. I am a cripple. I choose this word to name me. I choose from among several possibilities, the most common of which are *handicapped* and *disabled*. I made the choice a number of years ago, without thinking, unaware of my motives for doing so. Even now, I'm not sure what those motives are, but I recognize that they are complex and not entirely flattering. People—crippled or not—wince at the word *cripple,* as they do not at *handicapped* or *disabled*. Perhaps I want them to wince. I want them to see me as a tough customer, one to whom the fates/gods/viruses have not been kind, but who can face the brutal truth of her existence squarely. As a cripple, I swagger.

But, to be fair to myself, a certain amount of honesty underlies my choice. *Cripple* seems to me a clean word, straightforward and precise. It has an honorable history, having made its first appearance in the Lindisfarne Gospel in the tenth century. As a lover of words, I like the accuracy with which it describes my condition: I have lost the full use of my limbs. *Disabled,* by contrast, suggests any incapacity, physical or mental. And I certainly don't like *handicapped,* which implies that I have deliberately been put at a disadvantage, by whom I can't imagine (my God is not a Handicapper General), in order to equalize chances in the great race of life. These words seem to me to be moving away from my condition, to be widening the gap between word and reality. Most remote is the recently coined euphemism *differently abled,* which partakes of the same semantic hopefulness that transformed countries from *undeveloped* to *underdeveloped,* then to *less developed,* and finally to *developing* nations. People have continued to starve in those countries during the shift. Some realities do not obey the dictates of language.

Mine is one of them. Whatever you call me, I remain crippled. But I don't care what I am called, as long as it isn't *differently abled,* which strikes me as pure verbal garbage designed, by its ability to describe anyone, to describe no one. I subscribe to George Orwell's thesis that "the sloppiness of our language makes it easier for us to have foolish thoughts." And I refuse to participate in the degeneration of the language to the extent that I deny that I have lost anything in the course of this calamitous disease; I refuse to pretend that the only differences between you and me are the various ordinary ones that distinguish any one person from another. But call me *disabled* or *handicapped* if you like. I have long since grown accustomed to them; and if they are vague, at least they hint at the truth. Moreover, I use them myself. Society is no readier to accept crippledness than to accept death, war, sex, sweat, or wrinkles. I would never refer to another person as a cripple. It is the word I use to name only myself.

I haven't always been crippled, a fact for which I am soundly grateful. To be whole of limb is, I know from experience, infinitely more pleasant and useful than to be crippled; and if that knowledge leaves me open to bitterness at my loss, the physical soundness I once enjoyed (though I did not enjoy it half enough) is well worth the occasional stab of regret. Though never any good at sports, I was a normally active child and young adult. I climbed trees, played hopscotch, jumped rope, skated, swam, rode my bicycle, sailed. I despised team sports, spending some of the most wretched afternoons of my life, sweaty and humiliated, behind a field-hockey stick and under a basketball hoop. I tramped alone for miles along the bridle paths that webbed the woods behind the house I grew up in. I swayed through countless dim hours in the arms of one man or another under the scattered shot of light from mirrored balls, and gyrated through countless more as Tab Hunter and Johnny Mathis gave way to the Rolling Stones, Creedence Clearwater Revival, Cream. I walked down the aisle. I pushed baby carriages, changed tires in the rain, marched for peace.

When I was twenty-nine, I started to trip and drop things. What at first seemed my natural clumsiness soon became too pronounced to shrug off. I consulted a neurologist, who told me that I had a brain tumor. A battery of tests, increasingly disagreeable, revealed no tumor. About a year and a half later I developed a blurred spot in one eye. I had, at last, the episodes "disseminated in space and time" requisite for a diagnosis: multiple sclerosis. I have never been sorry for the doctor's initial misdiagnosis, however. For almost a week, until the negative results of the tests were in, I thought that I was going to die right away. Every day for the past nearly ten years, then, has been a kind of gift. I accept all gifts.

Multiple sclerosis is a chronic degenerative disease of the central nervous system, in which the myelin that sheathes the nerves is somehow eaten away and scar tissue forms in its place, interrupting the nerves' signals. During its course, which is unpredictable and uncontrollable, one may lose vision, hearing, speech, the ability to walk, control of bladder and/or bowels, strength in any or all extremities, sensitivity to touch, vibration, and/or pain, potency, coordination of movements—the list of possibilities is lengthy and horrifying. One may also lose one's sense of humor. That's the easiest to lose and the hardest to survive without.

In the past ten years, I have sustained some of these losses. Characteristic of MS are sudden attacks, called exacerbations, followed by remissions, and these I have not had. Instead, my disease has been slowly progressive. My left leg is now so weak that I walk with the aid of a brace and a cane; and for distances I use an Amigo, a variation on the electric wheelchair that looks rather like an electrified kiddie car. I no longer have much use of my left hand. Now my right side is weakening as well. I still have the blurred spot in my right eye. Overall, though, I've been lucky so far. My world has, of necessity, been circumscribed by my losses, but the terrain left me has been ample enough for me to continue many of the activities that absorb me: writing, teaching, raising children and cats and plants and snakes, reading, speaking publicly about MS and depression, even playing bridge with people patient and honorable enough to let me scatter cards every which way without sneaking a peek.

Lest I begin to sound like Pollyanna, however, let me say that I don't like having MS. I hate it. My life holds realities—harsh ones, some of them—that no right-minded human being ought to accept without grumbling. One of them is fatigue. I know of no one with MS who does not complain of bone-weariness; in a disease that presents an astonishing variety of symptoms, fatigue seems to be a common factor. I wake up in the morning feeling the way most people do at the end of a bad day, and I take it from there. As a result, I spend a lot of time *in extremis* and, impatient with limitation, I tend to ignore my fatigue until my body breaks down in some way and forces rest. Then I miss picnics, dinner parties, poetry readings, the brief visits of old friends from out of town. The offspring of a puritanical tradition of exceptional venerability, I cannot view these lapses without shame. My life often seems a series of small failures to do as I ought.

I lead, on the whole, an ordinary life, probably rather like the one I would have led had I not had MS. I am lucky that my predilections were already solitary, sedentary, and bookish—unlike the world-famous French cellist I have read about, or the young woman I talked with one long afternoon who wanted only to be a jockey. I had just begun graduate school when I found out something was wrong with me, and I have remained—interminably—a graduate student. Perhaps I would not have if

I'd thought I had the stamina to return to a full-time job as a technical editor; but I've enjoyed my studies.

In addition to studying, I teach writing courses. I also teach medical students how to give neurological examinations. I pick up free-lance editing jobs here and there. I have raised a foster son and sent him into the world, where he has made me two grandbabies, and I am still escorting my daughter and son through adolescence. I go to mass every Saturday. I am a superb, if messy, cook. I am also an enthusiastic laundress, capable of sorting a hamper full of clothes into five subtly differentiated piles, but a terrible housekeeper. I can do italic writing and, in an emergency, bathe an oil-soaked cat. I play a fiendish game of Scrabble. When I have the time and the money, I like to sit on my front steps with my husband, drinking Amaretto and smoking a cigar, as we imagine our counterparts in Leningrad and make sure that the sun gets down once more behind the sharp childish scrawl of the Tucson mountains.

This lively plenty has its bleak complement, of course, in all the things I can no longer do. I will never run again, except in dreams, and one day I may have to write that I will never walk again. I like to go camping, but I can't follow George and the children along the trails that wander out of a campsite through the desert or into the mountains. In fact, even on the level I've learned never to check the weather or try to hold a coherent conversation: I need all my attention for my wayward feet. Of late, I have begun to catch myself wondering how people can propel themselves without canes. With only one usable hand, I have to select my clothing with care not so much for style as for ease of ingress and egress, and even so, dressing can be laborious. I can no longer do fine stitchery, pick up babies, play the piano, braid my hair. I am immobilized by acute attacks of depression, which may or may not be physiologically related to MS but are certainly its logical concomitant.

These two elements, the plenty and the privation, are never pure, nor are the delight and wretchedness that accompany them. Almost every pickle that I get into as a result of my weakness and clumsiness—and I get into plenty—is funny as well as maddening and sometimes painful. I recall one May afternoon when a friend and I were going out for a drink after finishing up at school. As we were climbing into opposite sides of my car, chatting, I tripped and fell, flat and hard, onto the asphalt parking lot, my abrupt departure interrupting him in mid-sentence. "Where'd you go?" he called as he came around the back of the car to find me hauling myself up by the door frame. "Are you all right?" Yes, I told him, I was fine, just a bit rattly, and we drove off to find a shady patio and some beer. When I got home an hour or so later, my daughter greeted me with, "What have you done to yourself?" I looked down. One elbow of my white turtleneck with the green froggies, one knee of my white trousers, one white kneesock were blood-soaked. We peeled off the clothes and inspected the damage, which was nasty enough but not alarming. That part wasn't funny: The abrasions took a long time to heal, and one got a little infected. Even so, when I think of my friend talking earnestly, suddenly, to the hot thin air while I dropped from his view as though through a trap door, I find the image as silly as something from a Marx Brothers movie.

I may find it easier than other cripples to amuse myself because I live propped by the acceptance and the assistance and, sometimes, the amusement of those around me. Grocery clerks tear my checks out of my checkbook for me, and sales clerks find chairs to put into dressing rooms when I want to try on clothes. The people I work with make sure I teach at times when I am least likely to be fatigued, in places I can get to, with the materials I need. My students, with one anonymous exception (in an end-of-the-semester evaluation), have been unperturbed by my disability. Some even like it. One was immensely cheered by the information that I paint my own fingernails; she decided, she told me, that if I could go to such trouble over fine details, she could keep on writing essays. I suppose I became some sort of bright-fingered muse. She wrote good essays, too.

The most important struts in the framework of my existence, of course, are my husband and children. Dismayingly few marriages survive the MS test, and why should they? Most twenty-two- and nineteen-year-olds, like George and me, can vow in clear conscience, after a childhood of chicken pox and summer colds, to keep one another in sickness and in health so long as they both shall live. Not many are equipped for catastrophe: the dismay, the depression, the extra work, the boredom that a degenerative disease can insinuate into a relationship. And our society, with its emphasis on fun and its association of fun with physical performance, offers little encouragement for a whole spouse to stay with a crippled partner. Children experience similar stresses when faced with a crippled parent, and they are more helpless, since parents and children can't usually get divorced. They hate, of course, to be different from their peers, and the child whose mother is tacking down the aisle of a school auditorium packed with proud parents like a Cape Cod dinghy in a stiff breeze jolly well stands out in a crowd. Deprived of legal divorce, the child can at least deny the mother's disability, even her existence, forgetting to tell her about recitals and PTA meetings, refusing to accompany her to stores or church or the movies, never inviting friends to the house. Many do.

But I've been limping along for ten years now, and so far George and the children are still at my left elbow, holding tight. Anne and Matthew vacuum floors and dust furniture and haul trash and rake up dog droppings and button my cuffs and bake lasagna and Toll House cookies with just enough grumbling so I know that they don't have brain fever. And far from hiding me, they're forever dragging me by racks of fancy clothes or through teeming school corridors, or welcoming gaggles of friends while I'm wandering through the house in Anne's filmy pink babydoll pajamas.

George generally calls before he brings someone home, but he does just as many dumb thankless chores as the children. And they all yell at me, laugh at some of my jokes, write me funny letters when we're apart—in short, treat me as an ordinary human being for whom they have some use. I think they like me. Unless they're faking. . . .

Faking. There's the rub. Tugging at the fringes of my consciousness always is the terror that people are kind to me only because I'm a cripple. My mother almost shattered me once, with that instinct mothers have—blind, I think, in this case, but unerring nonetheless—for striking blows along the fault-lines of their children's hearts, by telling me, in an attack on my selfishness, "We all have to make allowances for you, of course, because of the way you are." From the distance of a couple of years, I have to admit that I haven't any idea just what she meant, and I'm not sure that she knew either. She was awfully angry. But at the time, as the words thudded home, I felt my worst fear suddenly realized. I could bear being called selfish: I am. But I couldn't bear the corroboration that those around me were doing in fact what I'd always suspected them of doing, professing fondness while silently they put up with me because of the way I am. A cripple. I've been a little cracked ever since.

Along with this fear that people are secretly accepting shoddy goods comes a relentless pressure to please—to prove myself worth the burdens I impose, I guess, or to build a substantial account of good will against which I may write drafts in times of need. Part of the pressure arises from social expectations. In our society, anyone who deviates from the norm had better find some way to compensate. Like fat people, who are expected to be jolly, cripples must bear their lot meekly and cheerfully. A grumpy cripple isn't playing by the rules. And much of the pressure is self-generated. Early on I vowed that, if I had to have MS, by God I was going to do it well. This is a class act, ladies and gentlemen. No tears, no recriminations, no faintheartedness.

One way and another, then, I wind up feeling like Tiny Tim, peering over the edge of the table at the Christmas goose, waving my crutch, piping down God's blessing on us all. Only sometimes I don't want to play Tiny Tim. I'd rather be Caliban, a most scurvy monster. Fortunately, at home no one much cares whether I'm a good cripple or a bad cripple so long as I make vichyssoise with fair regularity. One evening several years ago, Anne was at the diningroom table reading while I cooked dinner. As I opened a can of tomatoes, the can slipped in my left hand and juice spattered me and the counter with bloody spots. Fatigued and infuriated, I bellowed, "I'm so sick of being crippled. . . . " Anne glanced at me over the top of her book. "There now," she said, "do you feel better?" "Yes," I said, "yes I do." She went back to her reading. I felt better. That's about all the attention my scurviness ever gets.

Because I hate being crippled, I sometimes hate myself for being a cripple. Over the years I have come to expect—even accept—attacks of violent self-loathing. Luckily, in general our society no longer connects deformity and disease directly with evil (though a charismatic once told me that I have MS because a devil is in me) and so I am allowed to move largely at will, even among small children. But I'm not sure that this revision of attitude has been particularly helpful. Physical imperfection, even freed of moral disapprobation, still defines and violates the ideal, especially for women, whose confinement in their bodies as objects of desire is far from over. Each age, of course, has its ideal, and I doubt that ours is any better or worse than any other. Today's ideal woman, who lives on the glossy pages of dozens of magazines, seems to be between the ages of eighteen and twenty-five; her hair has body, her teeth flash white, her breath smells minty, her underarms are dry; she has a career but is still a fabulous cook, especially of meals that take less than twenty minutes to prepare; she does not ordinarily appear to have a husband or children; she is trim and deeply tanned; she jogs, swims, plays tennis, rides a bicycle, sails, but does not bowl; she travels widely, even to out-of-the-way places like Finland and Samoa, always in the company of the ideal man, who possesses a nearly identical set of characteristics. There are a few exceptions. Though usually white and often blonde, she may be black, Hispanic, oriental, or native American, so long as she is unusually sleek. She may be old, provided she is selling a laxative or is Lauren Bacall. If she is selling a detergent, she may be married and have a flock of strikingly messy children. But she is never a cripple.

Like many women I know, I have always had an uneasy relationship with my body. I was not a popular child, largely, I think now, because I was peculiar; intelligent, intense, moody, shy, given to unexpected actions and inexplicable notions and emotions. But as I entered adolescence, I believed myself unpopular because I was homely: my breasts too flat, my mouth too wide, my hips too narrow, my clothing never quite right in fit or style. I was not, in fact, particularly ugly, old photographs inform me, though I was well off the ideal; but I carried this sense of self-alienation with me into adulthood, where it regenerated in response to the depradations of MS. Even with my brace I walk with a limp so pronounced that, seeing myself on the videotape of a television program on the disabled, I couldn't believe that anything but an inchworm could make progress humping along like that. My shoulders droop and my pelvis thrusts forward as I try to balance myself upright, throwing my frame into a bony S. As a result of contractures, one shoulder is higher than the other and I carry one arm bent in front of me, the fingers curled into a claw. My left arm and leg have wasted into pipe-stems, and I try always to keep them covered. When I think about how my body must look to others, especially to men, to whom I have been trained to display myself, I feel ludicrous, even loathsome.

At my age, however, I don't spend much time thinking about my appearance. The burning egocentricity of adolescence, which assures one that all the world is looking all the time, has passed, thank God, and I'm generally too caught up in what I'm doing to step back, as I used to, and watch myself as though upon a stage. I'm also too old to believe in the accuracy of self-image. I know that I'm not a hideous crone, that in fact, when I'm rested, well dressed, and well made up, I look fine. The self-loathing I feel is neither physically nor intellectually substantial. What I hate is not me but a disease.

I am not a disease.

And a disease is not—at least not singlehandedly—going to determine who I am, though at first it seemed to be going to. Adjusting to a chronic incurable illness, I have moved through a process similar to that outlined by Elizabeth Kübler-Ross in *Death and Dying*. The major difference—and it is far more significant than most people recognize—is that I can't be sure of the outcome, as the terminally ill cancer patient can. Research studies indicate that, with proper medical care, I may achieve a "normal" life span. And in our society, with its vision of death as the ultimate evil, worse even than decrepitude, the response to such news is, "Oh, well, at least you're not going to *die*."

Are there worse things than dying? I think there may be.

I think of two women I know, both with MS, both enough older than I to have served me as models. One took to her bed several years ago and has been there ever since. Although she can sit in a high-backed wheelchair, because she is incontinent she refuses to go out at all, even though incontinence pants, which are readily available at any pharmacy, could protect her from embarrassment. Instead, she stays at home and insists that her husband, a small quiet man, a retired civil servant, stay there with her except for a quick weekly foray to the supermarket. The other woman, whose illness was diagnosed when she was eighteen, a nursing student engaged to a young doctor, finished her training, married her doctor, accompanied him to Germany when he was in the service, bore three sons and a daughter, now grown and gone. When she can, she travels with her husband; she plays bridge, embroiders, swims regularly; she works, like me, as a symptomatic patient instructor of medical students in neurology.

Guess which woman I hope to be.

At the beginning, I thought about having MS almost incessantly. And because of the unpredictable course of the disease, my thoughts were always terrified. Each night I'd get into bed wondering whether I'd get out again the next morning, whether I'd be able to see, to speak, to hold a pen between my fingers. Knowing that the day might come when I'd be physically incapable of killing myself, I thought perhaps I ought to do so right away, while I still had the strength. Gradually I came to understand that the Nancy who might one day lie inert under a bedsheet, arms and legs paralyzed, unable to feed or bathe herself, unable to reach out for a gun, a bottle of pills, was not the Nancy I was at present, and that I could not presume to make decisions for that future Nancy, who might well not want in the least to die. Now the only provision I've made for the future Nancy is that when the time comes—and it is likely to come in the form of pneumonia, friend to the weak and the old—I am not to be treated with machines and medications. If she is unable to communicate by then, I hope she will be satisfied with these terms.

Thinking all the time about having MS grew tiresome and intrusive, especially in the large and tragic mode in which I was accustomed to considering my plight. Months and even years went by without catastrophe (at least without one related to MS), and really I was awfully busy, what with George and children and snakes and students and poems, and I hadn't the time, let alone the inclination, to devote myself to being a disease. Too, the richer my life became, the funnier it seemed, as though there were some connection between largesse and laughter, and so my tragic stance began to waver until, even with the aid of a brace and a cane, I couldn't hold it for very long at a time.

After several years I was satisfied with my adjustment. I had suffered my grief and fury and terror, I thought, but now I was at ease with my lot. Then one summer day I set out with George and the children across the desert for a vacation in California. Part way to Yuma I became aware that my right leg felt funny. "I think I've had an exacerbation," I told George. "What shall we do?" he asked. "I think we'd better get the hell to California," I said, "because I don't know whether I'll ever make it again." So we went on to San Diego and then to Orange, up the Pacific Coast Highway to Santa Cruz, across to Yosemite, down to Sequoia and Joshua Tree, and so back over the desert to home. It was a fine two-week trip, filled with friends and fair weather, and I wouldn't have missed it for the world, though I did in fact make it back to California two years later. Nor would there have been any point in missing it, since in MS, once the symptoms have appeared, the neurological damage has been done, and there's no way to predict or prevent that damage.

The incident spoiled my self-satisfaction, however. I renewed my grief and fury and terror, and I learned that one never finishes adjusting to MS. I don't know now why I thought one would. One does not, after all, finish adjusting to life, and MS is simply a fact of my life—not my favorite fact, of course—but as ordinary as my nose and my tropical fish and my yellow Mazda station wagon. It may at any time get worse, but no amount of worry or anticipation can prepare me for a new loss. My life is a lesson in losses. I learn one at a time.

And I had best be patient in the learning, since I'll have to do it like it or not. As any rock fan knows, you can't always get what you want. Particularly when you have MS. You can't, for example, get cured. In recent years researchers and the organizations that fund research have started to pay MS some attention even though it isn't fatal; perhaps they have begun to see that life is something other than a quantitative phenomenon, that one may be very much alive for a very long time in a life that isn't worth living. The researchers have made some progress toward understanding the mechanism of the disease: It may well be an autoimmune reaction triggered by a slow-acting virus. But they are nowhere near its prevention, control, or cure. And most of us want to be cured. Some, unable to accept incurability, grasp at one treatment after another, no matter how bizarre: megavitamin therapy, gluten-free diet, injections of cobra venom, hypothermal suits, lymphocytopharesis, hyperbaric chambers. Many treatments are probably harmless enough, but none are curative.

The absence of a cure often makes MS patients bitter toward their doctors. Doctors are, after all, the priests of modern society, the new shamans, whose business is to heal, and many MS patients rove from one to another, searching for the "good" doctor who will make them well. Doctors too think of themselves as healers, and for this reason many have trouble dealing with MS patients, whose disease in its intransigence defeats their aims and mocks their skills. Too few doctors, it is true, treat their patients as whole human beings, but the reverse is also true. I have always tried to be gentle with my doctors, who often have more at stake in terms of ego than I do. I may be frustrated, maddened, depressed by the incurability of my disease, but I am not diminished by it, and they are. When I push myself up from my seat in the waiting room and stumble toward them, I incarnate the limitation of their powers. The least I can do is refuse to press on their tenderest spots.

This gentleness is part of the reason that I'm not sorry to be a cripple. I didn't have it before. Perhaps I'd have developed it anyway—how could I know such a thing?—and I wish I had more of it, but I'm glad of what I have. It has opened and enriched my life enormously, this sense that my frailty and need must be mirrored in others, that in searching for and shaping a stable core in a life wrenched by change and loss, change and loss, I must recognize the same process, under individual conditions, in the lives around me. I do not deprecate such knowledge, however I've come by it.

All the same, if a cure were found, would I take it? In a minute. I may be cripple, but I'm only occasionally a loony and never a saint. Anyway, in my brand of theology God doesn't give bonus points for a limp. I'd take a cure; I just don't need one. A friend who also has MS startled me once by asking, "Do you ever say to yourself, 'Why me, Lord?' " "No, Michael, I don't," I told him, "because whenever I try, the only response I can think of is 'Why not?' " If I could make a cosmic deal, who would I put in my place? What in my life would I give up in exchange for sound limbs and a thrilling rush of energy? No one. Nothing. I might as well do the job myself. Now that I'm getting the hang of it.

Adrienne Rich

Transit

When I meet the skier she is always
walking, skis and poles shouldered, toward the mountain
knee-swinging in worn boots
over the path new-sifted with fresh snow
over greying dark hair almost hidden by
a cap of many colors
her fifty-year-old, strong, impatient body
dressed for cold and speed
her eyes level with mine

And when we pass each other I look into her face
wondering what we have in common
where our minds converge
for we do not pass each other, she passes me
as I halt beside the fence tangled in snow,
she passes me as I shall never pass her
in this life

Yet I remember us together
climbing Chocorua, summer nineteen-forty-five
details of vegetation beyond the timberline
lichens, wildflowers, birds,
amazement when the trail broke out onto the granite ledge
sloped over blue lakes, green pines, giddy air
like dreams of flying

When sisters separate they haunt each other
as she, who I might once have been, haunts me
or is it I who do the haunting
halting and watching on the path
how she appears again through lightly-blowing
crystals, how her strong knees carry her,
how unaware she is, how simple
this is for her, how without let or hindrance
she travels in her body
until the point of passing, where the skier
and the cripple must decide
to recognize each other?

from The Body's Memory

I've just shown Peter this journal. His idea, not mine; he says that as my—or rather, as the journal's—Official Muse, he has the right to see it.

An acidulous muse, to be sure. His first comment: "So why did you stop? It's been more than eight years! Quit fuckin' around and finish it!"

(He's flattered, he says, by the depiction of himself. Especially "that stuff about the broad back.")

"How will I know when it's 'finished'?"

"It may never be 'finished.' But at least you could set the record straight about your pills. We did give them back to you, remember?" Turning toward me to bat a mosquito, his sunglasses reflecting two tiny images of me beside him, he adds, "Write about your move. Write about living alone."

He stretches his legs. My oldest friend (with Ellen), he sits in a folding canvas chair beside my wheelchair, in my postage-stamp surburban back yard. A splendid old willow tree squats beside us, its fronds drooping in our laps, covered with cottony wads of seeds that drift in the air like lazy snow. Off in a corner of the yard is my little vegetable garden, which Ellen planted and which she tends weekly in her rolled-up jeans and straw hat with the limp frayed edges that remind me of my willow fronds.

The reference to pills holds me for a moment. Eight years ago, after my last tumor surgery, Peter and Ellen hid both bottles (sleeping pills and painkillers), convinced I would down them all, as I'd been known to do on previous occasions when my life hit bottom. Since movement was difficult for me then, and since my friends tended me round the clock, the pills were safe in their hiding place and I lived to see this sunny day with Peter in my yard. For I do believe they were right . . .

Why *did* I stop keeping the journal? After moving out of Ellen's—and out of my old apartment with its two flights of stairs—I think I lost the sense of urgency that originally impelled me to write things down. At Ellen's, and surely before that, in the hospital, I felt so demeaningly helpless and found myself so constantly surrounded by people that journal-keeping—along with certain other acts of defiance like unplugging my phone—afforded me my only shreds of privacy and self-assertion. Privacy in my new life became a more thunderous presence than the most obstreperous roommates or visitors. And the demands of living alone preoccupied me, so that journal-keeping seemed a luxury.

I rested in my yard often that first summer, sometimes facing in toward the house so I could look through the back windows—one full wall of the house—to the quiet sleepy living room within. Seen from outside it had a dreamlike quality: so bright and calm a space after such dark chaos. Often I was not sure which was the dream, this well-ordered little patch of light or the darkness that preceded it.

Nighttimes were particularly confusing: when sunlight faded from the rooms, and my leg was dizzy with pain from trying to pretend it could do anything, and I crawled between the sheets and the bed stretched round me, vast and empty as a desert, I felt that other darkness encroaching on the sturdy, safe daytime world. It was hard not to panic, then.

I did seem to be proving what I'd set out to prove: that I could live alone. The question began to modify itself: *should* I, given the cost?

My doubters were legion. Even Ellen—whose kitchen wall at the time sported a blown-up photo of her favorite (Parisian) graffiti, "SOYEZ REALISTES: EXIGEZ L'IMPOSSIBLE!" ("Be Realistic: Demand the Impossible!")—even Ellen was uneasy. When a suitable accessible place was finally found and moving day was imminent, she sat me down in my new, bare kitchen and said, "Jen, let's talk cooking."

(She wanted, she said, to "put me through my paces.")

"How will you chop vegetables?"

"I'll sit at the counter on a stool." (I was using Canadian crutches at the time.)

"Show me."

"How can I? There's no stool."

Swatting aside my objection with an elaborate "Why me, Lord?" look, she started to clamber onto an imaginary stool, whacking her knees ostentatiously against the lower cupboards.

"Hmmm. Okay, so the kitchen needs a few adaptations. Maybe the landlord . . ."

"How will you set the table?"

"I'll put everything on one of those little carts with wheels and roll it into the dining room."

"How will you move the cart?"

Silence. "Push it with my feet?"

"It'll be too hard to roll on these rough floor boards. Better stick to the kitchen table and forget about the dining room."

"But how will I set the kitchen table?"

And so on.

During those first few weeks I did in fact confine my meals to the kitchen table, which I managed to set by passing dishes from cupboard to counter to table while sitting on my stool. I also improvised a technique that became for some time my basic—if graceless—method of propulsion around the kitchen: abandoning crutches, I'd grab the sink or counter and drag myself like a twenty-five-pound sack of cat kibble.

Then I discovered, to my amazement, that with some lurching and teeth-gritting I could walk with *one* crutch for a few feet, freeing my right hand to carry things. Triumph! I began to eat my solitary suppers at the dining table, complete with placemat and stemmed wineglass. In the end this one-crutch routine created many more problems than it solved, but I persisted for some time out of sheer stubborn "pride"—our culture calls it that—or, as Ellen would have it, masochism. In fact, it caused not only spectacular pain—the remaining muscles in my leg (calf, thigh, groin) being ill-equipped to do what I was demanding of them—but also possibly permanent damage to my spine (as I was to learn later). It was also shamefully clumsy; by the end of a few months nearly every dish I cherished had broken. But then, every system of mobility I've devised for myself in the past eight years of living with disability has been shamefully clumsy. The real effort has been twofold: to come to terms with my new gracelessness—I will never again be mistaken for a dancer—and to drop the word "shamefully" from its coupling with "clumsy."

Three full years of this nonsense with crutches lay ahead, before I would begin to accept the idea of using a wheelchair. That wheelchairs could be thought of as *conveniences* rather than as portable prisons, or worse, as badges of moral capitulation, was a life-transforming concept that simply did not occur to me.

"WHY?!" Ellen railed that day, confounded. "Why put yourself through this crap? Find a roommate! Get yourself a Sugar Daddy!—a Sugar *Parent*—to help you with the daily stuff."

"In exchange for services rendered?" I hissed.

"Jen, why are you always setting up tests, proving something to yourself? Life doesn't *have* to be so hard."

"Whose life?" A cheap shot, I knew. She'd paid her dues many times over.

Graciously she held her tongue; in time she dropped the roommate question. After all, she understood perfectly—as everyone who knew her knew—The Test, the need to be alone.

Coping mechanisms are boring, I tell Peter. Everyone copes, on one level or another. What interests me are other people's responses to my disability, which Peter and I have been jovially analyzing and grouping according to type, over Bloody Marys in my yard.

"There's the One-Foot-in-the-Grave mentality, first of all." He settles comfortably back, poking a scrap of lemon floating among his ice cubes. I'd given him one of my carnival-striped flexi-straws hoarded from hospital days, which he'd promptly removed with a disdainful curl of the lip.

" 'Now that your wings are clipped . . .' " I intone, mimicking the doleful sentimentality that is the hallmark of this group. We've found by comparing notes that the One-Foot-in-the-Gravers are more vocal around me; in fact Peter used to express amazement at the numerous strangers who commented on my disability, or commiserated with me, while I was getting about on forearm crutches.

Peter is almost never similarly approached. Apparently there is a newly disabled "look." Do people take his limp for granted because they cannot imagine him without it? While on crutches, I was invariably thought to be a sports accident "victim," skiing usually; Peter, on the other hand, is apparently assumed to have been born without legs. ("How gauche," he smiles.)

Those who've known me over the years and remember my past agility were for some time the most cloyingly morose; they did seem to believe they were witnessing the beginning of the end. Whereas strangers could be persuaded that my condition was stable, "old friends" stubbornly clung to their certainty that Death had me by the hand. I do still occasionally get pitying questions from strangers, though now that I no longer use crutches these are rare. Odd, that: It is as if wheelchairs are unspeakable. A public silence tends to surround my passage now wherever I go, causing me sometimes perversely to yearn for the old innocent nosiness. Most inquiries these days come from people who have not seen me since the advent of my tumor. Peter has reported sitting in on conversations that opened with something like: "I knew her when she used to chop firewood in Maine!"—as if documenting a Hollywood matinee idol's alcoholic decline. This would be followed by a curious kind of one-upmanship in which memories of Jen were traded for their athleticism!

"TACKY!" Ellen once crowed, recounting a similar dialogue overheard in the hospital waiting room. She'd sat quietly for some minutes before bringing the exchange to a rather hasty close by jumping up and cheerily exhorting the group: "Say, there's a sale on coffins this week, shall we all show our support by chipping in?"

The Healers are equally maddening. *"Faith,"* my young fruit-and-vegetable man solemnly intones. His large brown eyes meet mine for a moment before he resumes sweeping sawdust. He wears a tiny, pretty gold cross on a chain, nestled among his chest hairs, and an open-necked plaid shirt. "You'd be surprised . . ." he adds, and then lets it drop. "Here," rummaging through his fruit, "if you won't take my faith, at least take a bite of my banana."

There's something accusatory underlying even Dominic's disarming admonitions. "All you gotta do is believe, and live your life right" is not really so different from the pop psychologists who say that attitude is all. And it's everywhere, this view; scratch an apparently rational, well-informed citizen and lo, a Faith Healer is revealed. Even my goodhearted neighbor Beth once said to me, "If you convince yourself that you can do it, you'll be off those crutches in six months."

Ignorance? But Beth knew that I had very little hip muscle left, that muscle tissue does not regenerate, that the remaining muscles (calf and thigh) were already compensating as much as they were able, and that my one-crutch walking brought on murderous pain. Did she regard my pain threshold as that of a self-indulgent infant? Did she believe I'd sold myself a defeatist bill of goods? What about all my efforts to live independently, in defiance of all "sensible" advice?

There seems to be an inherent immorality, according to her view—poor Beth! I've scapegoated her, I know—in my principled acceptance of the fact of disability. Does God love crips only when they hate themselves, striving to be something they are not, disguising what they cannot change? I think of "reconstructive" breast surgery, even (in some cases) of prosthetic limbs, which Peter considers an uncomfortable nuisance, worse than no limbs at all. (But he's habituated to them, he says; he thinks he could not adapt to life in a wheelchair, at his age.)

Some years ago I embarrassed a concert hall full of people when a colleague from the staff of a magazine where I worked, having the best of intentions and the sensitivity of a slab of suet, approached me during intermission and eagerly urged me to pay a visit to a healing spa in New Mexico. I looked her in the eye and said, "What is it about me you would like to change?"

She drew back, offended. "Well, wouldn't you like to walk without crutches?"

A paragon of self-control, I contemplated a dozen or so bilious comebacks and said quietly, "I'm a little too busy for health spas." I was settling smugly back in my chair when a voice issued from somewhere near my bowels, "And besides," building with every syllable until it might have shattered glass, "WHAT THE HELL'S WRONG WITH CRUTCHES!"

"What the hell's wrong with compassion?" Peter's voice is sharp. "You're the one who called yourself 'helpless, dependent on the kindness of friends.' " He seizes the journal and, riffling through it, locates the offending passage.

I expected him fairly to hiccup with glee at this story. Irritably I play with my drink, holding up the glass so that the ice cubes glint in the sun. "I wrote that over eight years ago, in the hospital. I *was* helpless at the time, for Chrissake!"

"When you wrote that, you thought you'd always be helpless. You thought all disabled people are helpless."

"So big deal. I've changed. I'm smarter now."

"So look what you had to go through to get smart. Why can't you allow your friend to be a little dumber than you? She's where you were, five years ago. She hasn't had the same golden opportunities for growth," he adds drily.

"Look, when perfect strangers walk up to you on the street and say 'May I pray for you?' are you hearing an honest expression of compassion or are you being patronized?"

"Your friend is not a perfect stranger. Her motives were sincere," he lectures. "She saw you struggling with the crutches. Naturally she wanted to help. You can't fault people for that."

"I didn't 'struggle,' I *walked*. Anyway, crocodile tears," I glower, "are not my idea of compassion."

This is not what I mean to say. I don't want to argue; I want to tell him that disability was still new to me in those days, that all the way home from that concert I cried, raging, my grief a brand-new wound.

Peter is thoughtful; the cat, curled on his lap, crosses to mine and starts kneading my cut-off jeans. He is a victim of premature weaning, I tell myself; in fact I have no real reason to believe this fiction, the cat having been a foundling, but it does seem to enrapture him, this suckling on blankets, sweaters, whatever is at hand. Which shamelessly melts my heart.

Quietly Peter and I watch him now, like indulgent parents. Next to his little patch of wet denim is the bottom of my scar, a two-inch stretch peeking out from under my shorts. It's changed color by now; the raw meat look is gone, softened and faded by sun to a dusky purple-grey, the color of heather, of distant rolling Shenandoah mountains. I've come to like it, rather, I call it—how to explain this to Peter?—the color of *history*.

"It's hard," I blurt, interrupting my own reverie. "My disability is history now, I mean, I'm reconciled. Every time someone says 'I have a cure,' I do a doubletake: *A cure for what?* Not that I forget that I'm disabled, but I forget people think it's so bad. It always brings me up short. It's like they're trying to rip the scar open again."

Peter reaches over to pet the cat. His broad, hard-bit hands are rather battered for those of a guitarist. I love him for that. He's always complaining halfheartedly of broken nails. He has a way of sitting, slump-shouldered, neck thrust forward, that seems to apologize for itself at the same time as it issues a challenge. His knee joints used to look monstrous to me, poking through his trousers; now I forget they're there.

"Most folks mean no harm," he repeats gently. "You'll get used to them. They need educating, is all." He glances up at me and back down at the cat. "That's *our* job," he adds, and he touches the stray tag-end of scar sticking out of my jeans. A light, fleeting gesture. His fingers return to the cat.

"I'll do my teaching in the classroom!" I snap. "I'm busy, I have better things to do than . . ."

"Y'know, you're turning into a Bitter Nasty Ol' Crip!"

Bitter Nasty Ol' Crip is our code phrase, adapted from Ellen's proud, ironic mother, who coined it (Ellen says) in self-deprecation.

We smile. The air between us sighs. My cat stretches, yawns. Restless, I wheel the chair over to my vegetable garden—no small feat, wheeling on grass—and study it while Peter studies me. One more month and we'll be sinking our teeth into warm fat tomatoes. And Peter will watch the juice drip on my bare knees.

Peter likes me in shorts. His admiration notwithstanding, I refused to wear my cut-offs throughout most of that first summer. The scar seemed too ghoulish, snaking up over the waistband and down from the bottom of every pair of shorts I owned. By late July I broke down and even started wearing my bikini at the beach, often eliciting looks of curiosity, and occasionally, shock.

People apparently think they know what crips should look like. I startle them; I am clearly not helpless, not pathetic or sickly. A supermarket clerk who gave me a hand with my groceries last week confided that she'd gone against the advice of her boss, who had dramatically contended that I'd be offended by an offer of help. "She's an independent woman!" he'd proclaimed, having for some time watched my weekly battle with shopping carts, from his vantage point high up in the manager's booth.

Men seem particularly bemused by the sight of me, as if they expect disabled women to be asexual, as if they wish the scar were uglier, not so seamlessly a part of me. (Do most women have the same view of disabled men?) I am rarely harassed anymore—ah, the little fringe benefits—in bars or on the street. Back in the days when I was on crutches, men's stares at times suggested suspicion, as if the crutches might be nothing more than a sympathy ploy. (One beefy, watery-eyed fellow actually accused me outright. He withdrew his judgment when my friend the bartender suggested that an apology might be in order if he didn't "wanna get decked.")

Other men—not the supermarket manager—seem almost relieved, viewing my condition as license for unbridled chivalry. Tripping over themselves to open doors, clear paths, carry packages, they never fail to set in motion a welter of contrary emotions. I object to this kind of male fussing as I have objected since the dawn of my understanding of feminism; the difference is, now I often need their help. And loneliness prickles through my body like heat through not-quite-frostbitten toes.

With the advent of my wheelchair, much has changed. Many of the men who would have stared when I was using crutches now avert their eyes. Those brassy looks of sexual appraisal—men's eyes sweeping me from head to foot, sizing me up—happen much less frequently now. I had grown used to this behavior (which is not to say I found it acceptable), and come to expect it wherever I went. When I changed from crutches to wheelchair, something very curious happened to men's sexual interest in me. My Victorian Lit colleague at the university where I taught, who once confided to me that he thought a cane enhances a woman's femininity, assuredly does not think the same of wheelchairs. Women on crutches are still vertical figures, same general size and shape as other women, therefore the same species. Women seated in wheelchairs are short, their heads no higher than the average adult's chest, which makes them— significantly—the same height as kids. Their bodies are not so easy to assess, and one rarely gets a chance to watch them walk. The moment men identify my chair as a *wheelchair*— not so readily recognizable as most, being a dark, sleek little sports model quite unlike the clunky chrome tank-like medical models that dominate the market—their eyes slide away. It is as if, in that instant of recognition, I cease to exist for them as a sexual being. All their deepest fears and assumptions about "cripples" are summoned forth by the simple visual impact of my wheelchair.

One would think this change would have come as a relief to me, given how offensive I found the old "piece of ass" role. Perhaps partly because there's no real consistency—men do still undress me with their eyes, though less frequently and only after the initial shock has worn off—and partly because I clearly had internalized the old identity to some extent, I cannot say I've experienced the pleasure of such relief. On the contrary, I at first found myself suffering a kind of reflexive adolescent is-my-slip-showing? anxiety, regressing to the gawky eighth grader at the sock hop in 1959, who never got asked to dance by boys. This kind of reduction was too strange and uncomfortable to last very long; the more I exchanged notes with other disabled women, the easier it became to detach myself from old sexual values and to view them and their slavish adherents with a certain calm superiority. At first it was a hard and lonely private struggle, though, since at the time there were no disabled women in my circle of friends who could act as role models for me in terms of carving out for myself a new sexual identity. When I found them—disabled women, gay and straight, whose manner and bearing sent a clear message, i.e., *I know my own worth, and those who choose not to see it are the losers*—they served as beacons for me. My presence, my personal way of being in the world, underwent a subtle, life-transforming change.

It had to do with how they held their heads. How some women in manual chairs jumped curbs, practical, preoccupied with getting from here to there. (It was not the wheelies themselves; athleticism per se has no hold on me. It was that *style!*) How they entered rooms full of people, sitting straight, as if they had a right. How, breathing into their fat-ribbed respirator tubes, certain quadriplegic women paused to smile. How respirator breathing could seem suddenly sexy in a way that dragging on Virginia Slims never would, when at the end of that tube there flashed the briefest, most spectacular of smiles.

It was the Respirator Women who gave me permission to have a disability, whose casual grace finally shamed me into ownership. And with ownership came—at last—a wheelchair.

Days of Recovery

1.
All winter, nerves in my hip flaring,
my spine stiff, I've lain in bed,
a rubble of old magazines,
spring catalogs all around me.

How delicate healing is,
as if nothing were happening.

2.
The windows of my bedroom turn dark.
I watch neighbors' house lights
go on one by one. The circle closes:
knots of children in down parkas
come to tables set for supper,
husbands home from work,
striped ties loosened at their throats.
Down the street a station wagon
whines, then starts up. Once I could drive
into the city, talk poetry
with my good friends. I ate pastry
they brought from the *Eclair,*
spilled espresso during the argument
over line breaks. Tonight,
with my old companion, pain,
I look out at the lawns and houses.
Surely there are poems in this.

3.
My right hip aches where they took bone.
By lying flat

I can spend hours imagining
Emily Dickinson on her lonely garden walks,
letting her poems take over;
H.D.'s last sad days in a Swiss sanitorium,
and the purity of her late verse.
The only things I need now:

my hard bed, my yellow writing paper,
my red pen.

4.
Today I spot a cardinal pecking for seeds,
preening its ravaged feathers.
Soon misery will be over.
The fir tree bent from the ice will straighten.

But after this late March storm,
the buds are frozen,
the way my spine's rigid.
So many false beginnings.

5.
Good Friday,
masses of forsythia blaze through town.
In the park fishermen
are casting and reeling in the lake.
Everywhere the joy that comes
after long suffering.

It's now I dream of the morning
I'll wake without pain,
dress for celebration.
In my checked cap, red poplin jacket,
I'll walk into the back yard,
sniff the peppy air,
the sun warm on my neck.

The narcissi will be opening,
bud by bud.
Nothing can stop their blooming.

Deborah Kendrick

20/20 with a Twist

She swiveled her chair to face the desk again and absently slid the reference volume under the appropriate clamps of the dot-conversion deck. After ten years, it still seemed a minor miracle, she reflected, as the familiar process began with a nudge of the switch and a few adjustments of nobs. It was always a little thrilling to run her hand up the tactually blank page and feel the braille emerging magically. As chief administrator of the Department of Visual Equality, she found paper work and reference materials to be endless components of the job. The dot-converter made it all so effortless, so compact.

There were drawbacks to the device, of course. Since only 10 to 30 percent of the text could occupy a page at one time in its dot-converted form (due to the variations in space requirements), it could be a small irritation if the machine needed to be put in its reverse mode for recalling data that had already fled the page. Because of her age, however (she would be forty-seven on 05/04/2020), and the memories those years had incurred, Mary Seymour was not prone to viewing such annoyances with much seriousness. How could she, when the horrors of the nineties—those years now called "the dark ages for the visually impaired"—seemed like only yesterday?

She had been one of the lucky ones—learning to read prior to the silencing of braille. Even during her own childhood of the seventies and early eighties, braille teachers had been scarce. In the mid-eighties, university programs had ceased requiring braille for prospective teachers, and, with a reality more terrifying than any nightmare, braille production facilities had begun folding with rapid succession.

With the closing of radio reading service studios had gone access to print, to a large extent, and the withdrawal of special mailing privileges had taken most of what remained. By the 1990s, blind children were no longer being educated at all, and blind adults had begun to cluster together frantically for survival. Mary Seymour had been a teenager when the dark ages had become harsh reality, but she had tasted the joy of literacy and the freedom of movement sufficiently so that her role as revolutionary had never been a conscious decision. There had simply been no other logical alternative.

It had been a grim eighteen years—meeting with groups, large and small, in secrecy; teaching with outdated materials; plotting, failing, and finally success. Ironically, their greatest strength had been an element of visual impairment itself. Working without light, after all, was no real hardship for any of them.

Many tactics of the visionary rebellion, Mary reflected, had been comic, and many had been devastatingly effective. Tampering with power sources had been their greatest tool. First there had been the television blackout, allowing only audio portions of broadcasts nationwide to be transmitted. If her optic sensor had been installed during those days, Mary smiled, it might have been entertaining to see the faces of those in countless homes as TV screens first rolled and then went utterly blank.

"You, too, can function without pictures," the intermittent announcements had informed the seeing public. The rebels had scrambled computers, taken over radio networks, and then, tauntingly, ground all power to a halt. It had been a tedious struggle, but the gains had been remarkable.

A key to the success of the revolution had been its emphasis on peaceful tactics. No bodily harm had come to anyone on either side—unless, of course, one considered the capture of Mary and a dozen other revolutionary leaders or the optic sensor implantations as "bodily harm." The reasoning on the part of their captors had been along the lines that if the leadership of the visionary rebellion were transformed into seeing persons, they would automatically abandon the cause, and thus dissolve the movement. Some medical experimentation had been conducted prior to the dark ages in which mini-cameras had been connected to optic nerves, resulting in minimal vision for the totally blind. The optic sensor plan had been based on that earlier data, but weakly so, for the results were something of a surprise to all.

If there had ever been a moment when she had weighed the possibility of giving up the rebellion, it had been during the time of her capture. People moved wordlessly around the hospital bed where she had lain helplessly restrained. To Mary's repeated, although calm questions regarding their intentions, Mary was ultimately given the singular, short response: "You will see when the surgery is over." And so she had—in a manner of speaking.

The final power shut-down had enabled the dozen captives to escape three days following their imposed surgery. Only gradually in the months of negotiation ahead were they to realize what the effects—and the intended effects—of the implant operation had been. None were rendered seeing persons in the conventional sense, as had been intended, but each experienced some unexpected heightening awareness. George Thompson, for example, discovered a kind of telepathic effect, enabling him to form a visual image of a room before entering it. Joan Brighton realized that she could perceive colors. Mary Seymour's outcome was a bit more peculiar.

"I've always had an incredible hindsight," she had quipped in the final days of the visionary rebellion. Indeed, her own optic sensor—a typical follow-up of the implant exercise—provided her with a detailed visual perception of human faces and environments, but did so only after she had left their immediate vicinity. It was little more than a novelty now, rarely of any practical use. She did, however, occasionally attract attention to herself by entering an unfamiliar area, quickly and briefly retreating so that the image could establish itself in her mind, and then calmly re-entering. Usually the tools of her childhood were sufficient—sounds, smells, and the unconscious absorption of environmental cues through every cell of her body's surface.

The real success of the visionary rebellion had come in the form of print-accessing technology. Braille had been re-established in the universities in 2007, with far more stringent requirements than had ever existed previously. Visually impaired children were taught braille and print simultaneously, so that the choice was ultimately a personal one. Street signs, billboards, and elevators were all equipped with speech-synthesized devices. For those who used braille, dot-conversion decks were commonplace—desk models in offices for accessing books and computer information, and hand-held versions for quick reading of menus, entertainment programs, and similar materials. For the visually impaired print user, miniature high-powered magnifiers with polarity reversal mechanisms were the widespread answer to print accessibility.

Returning the reference volume to its place and noting that it was nearly time for her scheduled meeting with President Olga Henderson, Mary swiftly reviewed a few notes and switched off the converter. When she was a little girl, she thought, her teacher had told her that there were only two things that she could never do. "You will never drive an automobile," she had said, "and you will never read print."

Mary Seymour smiled with genuine contentment. Saint that she had been, even her teacher had underestimated the future of her visually impaired students. Private automobiles had been eliminated ten years ago now, so that the ability or inability of anyone to drive them was no longer relevant. As far as print was concerned, she thought, giving the converter an almost affectionate pat, she had something better than reading print: she could read everything, and read it in her own familiar language of dots.

Now where, she wondered with a touch of annoyance as she pushed back her chair, had she left the portfolio of data for the meeting with the President? Slipping into her coat, unfolding her white cane, Mary Seymour walked briskly out of the office and hesitated expectantly just beyond the threshold. With an impatient shake of her hair, she anticipated image finally flashed before her mind's eye.

"Ahh, yes," she said aloud as she hastily re-entered the office and snatched the portfolio from the top of the file cabinet. From the dark-age days of the nineties, the blind had finally achieved their long-deserved status in education and employment and had secured a Department of

Visual Equality in the bargain. The attractive woman who now strode confidently toward the elevators did not look much like a once tough-minded leader of the visionary rebellion. But, she thought, shifting the portfolio in her arm, she had the optic sensor as one amusing and occasionally useful souvenir.

"Going down," the elevator spoke in its distinct, synthesized syllables. The door slid open and, smiling, Mary Seymour stepped inside.

Muriel Rukeyser ————————————————

The Wards

St. George's Hospital, Hyde Park Corner

Lying in the moment, she climbs white snows;
At the foot of the bed the chart relates.
Here a man burns in fever; he is here, he is there,
Five thousand years ago in the cave country.
In this bed, I go wandering in Macao,
I run all night the black alleys. Time runs
Over the edge and all exists in all. We hold
All human history, all geography,
I cannot remember the word for what I need.
Our explorations, all at the precipice,
The night-table, a landscape of zebras,
Transistor constellations. All this music,
I heard it forming before I was born. I come
In this way, to the place.
                    Our selves lit clear,
This moment giving me necessity
Gives us ourselves and we risk everything,
Walking into our life.

Mary E. Wilkins Freeman

A Mistaken Charity

There were in a green field a little, low, weather-stained cottage, with a foot-path leading to it from the highway several rods distant, and two old women—one with a tin pan and old knife searching for dandelion greens among the short young grass, and the other sitting on the door-step watching her, or, rather, having the appearance of watching her.

"Air there enough for a mess, Harriét?" asked the old woman on the door-step. She accented oddly the last syllable of the Harriet, and there was a curious quality in her feeble, cracked old voice. Besides the question denoted by the arrangement of her words and the rising inflection, there was another, broader and subtler, the very essence of all questioning, in the tone of her voice itself; the cracked, quavering notes that she used reached out of themselves, and asked, and groped like fingers in the dark. One would have known by the voice that the old woman was blind.

The old woman on her knees in the grass searching for dandelions did not reply; she evidently had not heard the question. So the old woman on the door-step, after waiting a few minutes with her head turned expectantly, asked again, varying her question slightly, and speaking louder:

"Air there enough for a mess, do ye s'pose, Harriét?"

The old woman in the grass heard this time. She rose slowly and laboriously; the effort of straightening out the rheumatic old muscles was evidently a painful one; then she eyed the greens heaped up in the tin pan, and pressed them down with her hand.

"Wa'al, I don't know, Charlotte," she replied hoarsely. "There's plenty on 'em here, but I ain't got near enough for a mess; they do bile down so when you get 'em in the pot; an' it's all I can do to bend my j'ints enough to dig 'em."

"I'd give consider'ble to help ye, Harriét," said the old woman on the door-step.

But the other did not hear her; she was down on her knees in the grass again, anxiously spying out the dandelions.

So the old woman on the door-step crossed her little shrivelled hands over her calico knees, and sat quite still, with the soft spring wind blowing over her.

The old wooden door-step was sunk low down among the grasses, and the whole house to which it belonged had an air of settling down and mouldering into the grass as into its own grave.

When Harriet Shattuck grew deaf and rheumatic, and had to give up her work as tailoress, and Charlotte Shattuck lost her eyesight, and was unable to do any more sewing for her livelihood, it was a small and trifling charity for the rich man who held a mortgage on the little house in which they had been born and lived all their lives to give them the use of it, rent and interest free. He might as well have taken credit to himself for not charging a squirrel for his tenement in some old decaying tree in his woods.

So ancient was the little habitation, so wavering and mouldering, the hands that had fashioned it had lain still so long in their graves, that it almost seemed to have fallen below its distinctive rank as a house. Rain and snow had filtered through its roof, mosses had grown over it, worms had eaten it, and birds built their nests under its eaves; nature had almost completely overrun and obliterated the work of man, and taken her own to herself again, till the house seemed as much a natural ruin as an old tree-stump.

The Shattucks had always been poor people and common people; no especial grace and refinement or fine ambition had ever characterized any of them; they had always been poor and coarse and common. The father and his father before him had simply lived in the poor little house, grubbed for their living, and then unquestioningly died. The mother had been of no rarer stamp, and the two daughters were cast in the same mould.

After their parents' death Harriet and Charlotte had lived alone in the old place from youth to old age, with the one hope of ability to keep a roof over their heads, covering on their backs, and victuals in their mouths—an all-sufficient one with them.

Neither of them had ever had a lover; they had always seemed to repel rather than attract the opposite sex. It was not merely because they were poor, ordinary, and homely; there were plenty of men in the place who would have matched them well in that respect; the fault lay deeper—in their characters. Harriet, even in her girlhood, had a blunt, defiant manner that almost amounted to surliness, and was well calculated to alarm timid adorers, and Charlotte had always had the reputation of not being any too strong in her mind.

Harriet had gone about from house to house doing tailorwork after the primitive country fashion, and Charlotte had done plain sewing and mending for the neighbors. They had been, in the main, except when pressed by some temporary anxiety about their work or the payment thereof, happy and contented, with that negative kind of happiness and contentment which comes not from gratified ambition, but a lack of ambition itself. All that they cared for they had had in tolerable abundance, for Harriet at least had been swift and capable about her work. The patched, mossy old roof had been kept over their heads, the coarse, hearty food that they loved had been set on their table, and their cheap clothes had been warm and strong.

After Charlotte's eyes failed her, and Harriet had the rheumatic fever, and the little hoard of earnings went to the doctors, times were harder with them, though still it could not be said that they actually suffered.

When they could not pay the interest on the mortgage they were allowed to keep the place interest free; there was as much fitness in a mortgage on the little house, anyway, as there would have been on a rotten old apple-tree; and the people about, who were mostly farmers, and good friendly folk, helped them out with their living. One would donate a barrel of apples from his abundant harvest to the two poor old women, one a barrel of potatoes, another a load of wood for the winter fuel, and many a farmer's wife had bustled up the narrow foot-path with a pound of butter, or a dozen fresh eggs, or a nice bit of pork. Besides all this, there was a tiny garden patch behind the house, with a straggling row of currant bushes in it, and one of gooseberries, where Harriet contrived every year to raise a few pumpkins, which were the pride of her life. On the right of the garden were two old apple-trees, a Baldwin and a Porter, both yet in a tolerably good fruit-bearing state.

The delight which the two poor old souls took in their own pumpkins, their apples and currants, was indescribable. It was not merely that they contributed largely towards their living; they were their own, their private share of the great wealth of nature, the little taste set apart for them alone out of her bounty, and worth more to them on that account, though they were not conscious of it, than all the richer fruits which they received from their neighbors' gardens.

This morning the two apple-trees were brave with flowers, the currant bushes looked alive, and the pumpkin seeds were in the ground. Harriet cast complacent glances in their direction from time to time, as she painfully dug her dandelion greens. She was a short, stoutly built old woman, with a large face coarsely wrinkled, with a suspicion of a stubble of beard on the square chin.

When her tin pan was filled to her satisfaction with the sprawling, spidery greens, and she was hobbling stiffly towards her sister on the door-step, she saw another woman standing before her with a basket in her hand.

"Good-morning, Harriet," she said, in a loud, strident voice, as she drew near. "I've been frying some doughnuts, and I brought you over some warm."

"I've been tellin' her it was real good in her," piped Charlotte from the door-step, with an anxious turn of her sightless face towards the sound of her sister's footstep.

Harriet said nothing but a hoarse "Good-mornin,' Mis' Simonds." Then she took the basket in her hand, lifted the towel off the top, selected a doughnut, and deliberately tasted it.

"Tough," said she. "I s'posed so. If there is anything I 'spise on this airth it's a tough doughnut."

"Oh, Harriét!" said Charlotte, with a frightened look.

"They air tough," said Harriet, with hoarse defiance, "and if there is anything I 'spise on this airth it's a tough doughnut."

The woman whose benevolence and cookery were being thus ungratefully received only laughed. She was quite fleshy, and had a round, rosy, determined face.

"Well, Harriet," said she, "I am sorry they are tough, but perhaps you had better take them out on a plate, and give me my basket. You may be able to eat two or three of them if they are tough."

"They air tough—turrible tough," said Harriet, stubbornly; but she took the basket into the house and emptied it of its contents nevertheless.

"I suppose your roof leaked as bad as ever in that heavy rain day before yesterday?" said the visitor to Harriet, with an inquiring squint towards the mossy shingles, as she was about to leave with her empty basket.

"It was turrible," replied Harriet, with crusty acquiescence—"turrible. We had to set pails an' pans everywheres, an' move the bed out."

"Mr. Upton ought to fix it."

"There ain't any fix to it; the old ruff ain't fit to nail new shingles on to; the hammerin' would bring the whole thing down on our heads," said Harriet, grimly.

"Well, I don't know as it can be fixed, it's so old. I suppose the wind comes in bad around the windows and doors too?"

"It's like livin' with a piece of paper, or mebbe a sieve, 'twixt you an' the wind an' the rain," quoth Harriet, with a jerk of her head.

"You ought to have a more comfortable home in your old age," said the visitor, thoughtfully.

"Oh, it's well enough," cried Harriet, in quick alarm, and with a complete change of tone; the woman's remark had brought an old dread over her. "The old house'll last as long as Charlotte an' me do. The rain ain't so bad, nuther is the wind; there's room enough for us in the dry places, an' out of the way of the doors an' windows. It's enough sight better than goin' on the town." Her square, defiant old face actually looked pale as she uttered the last words and stared apprehensively at the woman.

"Oh, I did not think of your doing that," she said, hastily and kindly. "We all know how you feel about that, Harriet, and not one of us neighbors will see you and Charlotte go to the poorhouse while we've got a crust of bread to share with you."

Harriet's face brightened. "Thank ye, Mis' Simonds," she said, with reluctant courtesy. "I'm much obleeged to you an' the neighbors. I think mebbe we'll be able to eat some of them doughnuts if they air tough," she added, mollifyingly, as her caller turned down the foot-path.

"My, Harriét," said Charlotte, lifting up a weakly, wondering, peaked old face, "what did you tell her them doughnuts was tough fur?"

"Charlotte, do you want everybody to look down on us, an' think we ain't no account at all, just like beggars, 'cause they bring us in vittles?" said Harriet, with a grim glance at her sister's meek, unconscious face.

"No, Harriét," she whispered.

"Do you want *to go to the poor-house?*"

"No, Harriét." The poor little old woman on the door-step fairly cowered before her aggressive old sister.

"Then don't hender me agin when I tell folks their doughnuts is tough an' their pertaters is poor. If I don't kinder keep up an' show some sperrit, I shan't think nothing of myself, an' other folks won't nuther, and fust thing we know they'll kerry us to the poorhouse. You'd 'a been there before now if it hadn't been for me, Charlotte."

Charlotte looked meekly convinced, and her sister sat down on a chair in the doorway to scrape her dandelions.

"Did you git a good mess, Harriét?" asked Charlotte, in a humble tone.

"Toler'ble."

"They'll be proper relishin' with that piece of pork Mis' Mann brought in yesterday. O Lord, Harriét, it's a chink!"

Harriet sniffed.

Her sister caught with her sensitive ear the little contemptuous sound. "I guess," she said, querulously, and with more pertinacity than she had shown in the matter of the doughnuts, "that if you was in the dark, as I am, Harriét, you wouldn't make fun an' turn up your nose at chinks. If you had seen the light streamin' in all of a sudden through some little hole that you hadn't known of before when you set down on the door-step this mornin', and the wind with the smell of the apple blows in it came in your face, an' when Mis' Simonds brought them hot doughnuts, an' when I thought of the pork an' greens jest now—O Lord, how it did shine in! An' it does now. If you was me, Harriét, you would know there was chinks."

Tears began starting from the sightless eyes, and streaming pitifully down the pale old cheeks.

Harriet looked at her sister, and her grim face softened. "Why, Charlotte, hev it that thar *is* chinks if you want to. Who cares?"

"Thar *is* chinks, Harriét."

"Wa'al, thar *is* chinks, then. If I don't hurry, I sha'n't get these greens in in time for dinner."

When the two old women sat down complacently to their meal of pork and dandelion greens in their little kitchen they did not dream how destiny slowly and surely was introducing some new colors into their web of life, even when it was almost completed, and that this was one of the last meals they would eat in their old home for many a day. In about a week from that day they were established in the "Old Ladies' Home" in a neighboring city. It came about in this wise: Mrs. Simonds, the woman who had brought the gift of hot doughnuts, was a smart, energetic person, bent on doing good, and she did a great deal. To be sure, she always did it in her own way. If she chose to give hot doughnuts, she gave hot doughnuts; it made not the slightest difference to her if the recipients of her charity would infinitely have preferred ginger cookies. Still, a great many would like hot doughnuts, and she did unquestionably a great deal of good.

She had a worthy coadjustor in the person of a rich and childless elderly widow in the place. They had fairly entered into a partnership in good works, with about an equal capital on both sides, the widow furnishing the money, and Mrs. Simonds, who had much the better head of the two, furnishing the active schemes of benevolence.

The afternoon after the doughnut episode she had gone to the widow with a new project, and the result was that entrance fees had been paid, and old Harriet and Charlotte made sure of a comfortable home for the rest of their lives. The widow was hand in glove with officers of missionary boards and trustees of charitable institutions. There had been an unusual mortality among the inmates of the "Home" this spring, there were several vacancies, and the matter of the admission of Harriet and Charlotte was very quickly and easily arranged. But the matter which would have seemed the least difficult—inducing the two old women to accept the bounty which Providence, the widow, and Mrs. Simonds were ready to bestow on them—proved the most so. The struggle to persuade them to abandon their tottering old home for a better was a terrible one. The widow had pleaded with mild surprise, and Mrs. Simonds with benevolent determination; the counsel and reverend eloquence of the minister had been called in; and when they yielded at last it was with a sad grace for the recipients of a worthy charity.

It had been hard to convince them that the "Home" was not an almshouse under another name, and their yielding at length to anything short of actual force was only due probably to the plea, which was advanced most eloquently to Harriet, that Charlotte would be so much more comfortable.

The morning they came away, Charlotte cried pitifully, and trembled all over her little shrivelled body. Harriet did not cry. But when her sister had passed out the low, sagging door she turned the key in the lock, then took it out and thrust it slyly into her pocket, shaking her head to herself with an air of fierce determination.

Mrs. Simonds's husband, who was to take them to the depot, said to himself, with disloyal defiance of his wife's active charity, that it was a shame, as he helped the two distressed old souls into his light wagon, and put the poor little box, with their homely clothes in it, in behind.

Mrs. Simonds, the widow, the minister, and the gentleman from the "Home" who was to take charge of them, were all at the depot, their faces beaming with the delight of successful benevolence. But the two poor old women looked like two forlorn prisoners in their midst. It was an impressive illustration of the truth of the saying that "it is more blessed to give than to receive."

Well, Harriet and Charlotte Shattuck went to the "Old Ladies' Home" with reluctance and distress. They stayed two months, and then—they ran away.

The "Home" was comfortable, and in some respects even luxurious; but nothing suited those two unhappy, unreasonable old women.

The fare was of a finer, more delicately served variety than they had been accustomed to; those finely flavored nourishing soups for which the "Home" took great credit to itself failed to please palates used to common, coarser food.

"O Lord, Harriét, when I set down to the table here there ain't no chinks," Charlotte used to say. "If we could hev some cabbage, or some pork an' greens, how the light would stream in!"

Then they had to be more particular about their dress. They had always been tidy enough, but now it had to be something more; the widow, in the kindness of her heart, had made it possible, and the good folks in charge of the "Home," in the kindness of their hearts, tried to carry out the widow's designs.

But nothing could transform these two unpolished old women into two nice old ladies. They did not take kindly to white lace caps and delicate neckerchiefs. They liked their new black cashmere dresses well enough, but they felt as if they broke a commandment when they put them on every afternoon. They had always worn calico with long aprons at home, and they wanted to now; and they wanted to twist up their scanty gray locks into little knots at the back of their heads, and go without caps, just as they always had done.

Charlotte in a dainty white cap was pitiful, but Harriet was both pitiful and comical. They were totally at variance with their surroundings, and they felt it keenly, as people of their stamp always do. No amount of kindness and attention—and they had enough of both—sufficed to reconcile them to their new abode. Charlotte pleaded continually with her sister to go back to their old home.

"O Lord, Harriét," she would exclaim (by the way, Charlotte's "O Lord," which, as she used it, was innocent enough, had been heard with much disfavor in the "Home," and she, not knowing at all why, had been remonstrated with concerning it), "let us go home. I can't stay here no ways in this world. I don't like their vittles, an' I don't like to wear a cap; I want to go home and do different. The currants will be ripe, Harriét. O Lord, thar was almost a chink, thinking about 'em. I want some of 'em; an' the Porter apples will be gittin' ripe, an' we could have some apple-pie. This here ain't good; I want merlasses fur sweeting. Can't we get back no ways, Harriét? It ain't far, an' we could walk, an' they don't lock us in, nor nothin'. I don't want to die here; it ain't so straight up to heaven from here. O Lord, I've felt as if I was slantendicular from heaven ever since I've been here, an' it's been so awful dark. I ain't had any chinks. I want to go home, Harriét."

"We'll go to-morrow mornin,' " said Harriet, finally; "we'll pack up our things an' go; we'll put on our old dresses, an' we'll do up the new ones in bundles, an' we'll jest shy out the back way to-morrow morning'; an' we'll go. I kin find the way, an' I reckon we kin git thar, if it is fourteen mile. Mebbe somebody will give us a lift."

And they went. With a grim humor Harriet hung the new white lace caps with which she and Charlotte had been so pestered, one on each post at the head of the bedstead, so they would meet the eyes of the first person who opened the door. Then they took their bundles, stole slyly out, and were soon on the high-road, hobbling along, holding each other's hands, as jubilant as two children, and chuckling to themselves over their escape, and the probable astonishment there would be in the "Home" over it.

"O Lord, Harriét, what do you s'pose they will say to them caps?" cried Charlotte, with a gleeful cackle.

"I guess they'll see as folks ain't goin' to be made to wear caps agin their will in a free kentry," returned Harriet, with an echoing cackle, as they sped feebly and bravely along.

The "Home" stood on the very outskirts of the city, luckily for them. They would have found it a difficult undertaking to traverse the crowded streets. As it was, a short walk brought them into the free country road— free comparatively, for even here at ten o'clock in the morning there was considerable travelling to and from the city on business or pleasure.

People whom they met on the road did not stare at them as curiously as might have been expected. Harriet held her bristling chin high in air, and hobbled along with an appearance of being well aware of what she was about, that led folks to doubt their own first opinion that there was something unusual about the two old women.

Still their evident feebleness now and then occasioned from one and another more particular scrutiny. When they had been on the road a half-hour or so, a man in a covered wagon drove up behind them. After he had passed them, he poked his head around the front of the vehicle and looked back. Finally he stopped, and waited for them to come up to him.

"Like a ride, ma'am?" said he, looking at once bewildered and compassionate.

"Thankee," said Harriet, "we'd be much obleeged."

After the man had lifted the old women into the wagon, and established them on the back seat, he turned around, as he drove slowly along, and gazed at them curiously.

"Seems to me you look pretty feeble to be walking far," said he. "Where were you going?"

Harriet told him with an air of defiance.

"Why," he exclaimed, "it is fourteen miles out. You could never walk it in the world. Well, I am going within three miles of there, and I can go on a little farther as well as not. But I don't see— Have you been in the city?"

"I have been visitin' my married darter in the city," said Harriet, calmly. Charlotte started, and swallowed convulsively.

Harriet had never told a deliberate falsehood before in her life, but this seemed to her one of the tremendous exigencies of life which justify a lie. She felt desperate. If she could not contrive to deceive him in some way, the man might turn directly around and carry Charlotte and her back to the "Home" and the white caps.

"I should not have thought your daughter would have let you start for such a walk as that," said the man. "Is this lady your sister? She is blind, isn't she? She does not look fit to walk a mile."

"Yes, she's my sister," replied Harriet, stubbornly, "an' she's blind; an' my darter didn't want us to walk. She felt reel bad about it. But she couldn't help it. She's poor, and her husband's dead, an' she's got four leetle children."

Harriet recounted the hardships of her imaginary daughter with a glibness that was astonishing. Charlotte swallowed again.

"Well," said the man, "I am glad I overtook you, for I don't think you would ever have reached home alive."

About six miles from the city an open buggy passed them swiftly. In it were seated the matron and one of the gentlemen in charge of the "Home." They never thought of looking into the covered wagon—and indeed one can travel in one of those vehicles, so popular in some parts of New England, with as much privacy as he could in his tomb. The two in the buggy were seriously alarmed, and anxious for the safety of the old women, who were chuckling maliciously in the wagon they soon left far behind. Harriet had watched them breathlessly until they disappeared on a curve of the road; then she whispered to Charlotte.

A little after noon the two old women crept slowly up the foot-path across the field to their old home.

"The clover is up to our knees," said Harriet; "an' the sorrel and the white-weed; an' there's lots of yaller butterflies."

"O Lord, Harriét, thar's a chink, an' I do believe I saw one of them yaller butterflies go past it," cried Charlotte, trembling all over, and nodding her gray head violently.

Harriet stood on the old sunken door-step and fitted the key, which she drew triumphantly from her pocket, in the lock, while Charlotte stood waiting and shaking behind her.

Then they went in. Everything was there just as they had left it. Charlotte sank down on a chair and began to cry. Harriet hurried across to the window that looked out on the garden.

"The currants air ripe," said she; "an' them pumpkins hev run all over everything."

"O Lord, Harriét," sobbed Charlotte, "thar is so many chinks that they air all runnin' together!"

Mary E. Wilkins Freeman · 151

Vassar Miller ―――――――――――――――――――――

Love Song for Easter Even

Just for a moment now I feel immortal.
I lie on the grass with you. Its green awash
like seaweed under water. The long flash
of sky above us, blue jay's wing. Lush chortle
of birdsong in the leaves. No noise to startle,
but only soothe me here. I have no wish
to lie here still, with the sun's flush
light on my skin this way, forever gentle.

Just for a moment—hush, love!—I have quit
the binds and bonds of the body inside matter.
My bones are supple as a baby's—look!—my flesh
finds not a single flaw, seems infinite,
like Christ, can tread the tips of the grass like water.
Yet you dart past my touch like Him, smooth fish!

Alice Walker ―――――――――――――――――――――

Beauty: When the Other Dancer Is the Self

It is a bright summer day in 1947. My father, a fat, funny man with
beautiful eyes and a subversive wit, is trying to decide which of his eight
children he will take with him to the county fair. My mother, of course,
will not go. She is knocked out from getting us ready: I hold my neck stiff
against the pressure of her knuckles as she hastily completes the braiding
and then beribboning of my hair.

My father is the driver for the rich old white lady up the road. Her name
is Miss May. She owns all the land for miles around, as well as the house in
which we live. All I remember about her is that she once offered to pay
my mother 75 cents for cleaning her house, raking up piles of her magnolia leaves, and washing her family's clothes, and that my mother—she of

no money, eight children, and a chronic earache—refused it. But I do not think of this in 1947. I am two-and-a-half years old. I want to go everywhere my daddy goes. I am excited at the prospect of riding in a car. Someone has told me fairs are fun. That there is room in the car for only three of us doesn't faze me at all. Whirling happily in my starchy frock, showing off my biscuit polished patent leather shoes and lavender socks, tossing my head in a way that makes my ribbons bounce, I stand, hands on hips, before my father. "Take me, Daddy," I say with assurance, "I'm the prettiest!"

Later, it does not surprise me to find myself in Miss May's shiny black car, sharing the backseat with the other lucky ones. Does not surprise me that I thoroughly enjoy the fair. At home that night I tell all the unlucky ones about the merry-go-round, the man who eats live chickens, and the abundance of Teddy bears, until they say: that's enough, baby Alice. Shut up now, and go to sleep.

It is Easter Sunday, 1950. I am dressed in a green, flocked, scalloped-hem dress (handmade by my adoring sister Ruth) that has its own smooth satin petticoat and tiny hot-pink roses tucked into each scallop. My shoes, new T-strap patent leather, again highly biscuit polished. I am six years old and have learned one of the longest Easter speeches to be heard in church that day, totally unlike the speech I said when I was two: "Easter lilies/pure and white/blossom in/the morning light." When I rise to give my speech I do so on a great wave of love and pride and expectation. People in the church stop rustling their new crinolines. They seem to hold their breath. I can tell they admire my dress, but it is my spirit, bordering on sassiness (womanishness), they secretly applaud.

"That girl's a little mess," they whisper to each other, pleased.

Naturally I say my speech without stammer or pause, unlike those who stutter, stammer, or, worst of all, forget. This is before the word "beautiful" exists in people's vocabulary, but "Oh, isn't she the *cutest* thing!" frequently floats my way. *"And got so much sense!"* they gratefully add . . . for which thoughtful addition I thank them to this day.

It was great fun being cute. But then, one day, it ended.

I am eight years old and a tomboy. I have a cowboy hat, cowboy boots, checkered shirt and pants, all red. My playmates are my brothers, two and four years older than me. Their colors are black and green, the only difference in the way we are dressed. On Saturday nights we all go to the picture show, even my mother; Westerns are her favorite movies. Back home, "on the ranch," we pretend we are Tom Mix, Hopalong Cassidy, Lash LaRue (we've even named one of our dogs Lash LaRue); we chase each other for hours rustling cattle, being outlaws, delivering damsels from distress. Then my parents decide to buy my brothers guns. These are not "real" guns. They shoot "BBs," copper pellets my brothers say will kill birds. Because I am a girl, I do not get a gun. Instantly I am relegated to the position of Indian. Now there appears a great distance between us. They shoot and shoot at everything with their new guns. I try to keep up with my bow and arrows.

One day while I am standing on top of our makeshift "garage"—pieces of tin nailed across some poles—holding my bow and arrow and looking out toward the fields, I feel an incredible blow in my right eye. I look down just in time to see my brother lower his gun.

Both brothers rush to my side. My eye stings, and I cover it with my hand. "If you tell," they say, "we will get a whipping. You don't want that to happen, do you?" I do not. "Here is a piece of wire," says the older brother, picking it up from the roof, "say you stepped on one end of it and the other flew up and hit you." The pain is beginning to start. "Yes," I say. "Yes, I will say that is what happened." If I do not say thit is what happened, I know my brothers will find ways to make me wish I had. But now I will say anything that gets me to my mother.

Confronted by our parents we stick to the lie agreed upon. They place me on a bench on the porch and I close my left eye while they examine the right. There is a tree growing from underneath the porch, that climbs past the railing to the roof. It is the last thing my right eye sees. I watch as its trunk, its branches, and then its leaves are blotted out by the rising blood.

I am in shock. First there is intense fever, which my father tries to break using lily leaves bound around my head. Then there are chills: my mother tries to get me to eat soup. Eventually, I do not know how, my parents learn what has happened. A week after the "accident" they take me to see a doctor. "Why did you wait so long to come?" he asks, looking into my eye and shaking his head. "Eyes are sympathetic," he says. "If one is blind, the other will likely become blind too."

This comment of the doctor's terrifies me. But it is really how I look that bothers me most. Where the BB pellet struck there is a glob of whitish scar tissue, a hideous cataract, on my eye. Now when I stare at people—a favorite pastime, up to now—they will stare back. Not at the "cute" little girl, but at her scar. For six years I do not stare at anyone because I do not raise my head.

Years later, in the throes of a mid-life crisis, I ask my mother and sister whether I changed after the "accident." "No," they say, puzzled. "What do you mean?"

What do I mean?

I am eight, and for the first time, doing poorly in school, where I have been something of a whiz since I was four. We have just moved to the place where the "accident" occurred. We do not know any of the people around us because this is a different county. The only time I see the friends I knew is when we go back to our old church. My new school is the former state penitentiary. It is a large stone building, cold and drafty, crammed to overflowing with boisterous, ill-disciplined children. On the third floor there is a huge circular imprint of some partition that has been torn out.

"What used to be here?" I ask a sullen girl next to me on our way past it to lunch.

"The electric chair," says she.

At night I have nightmares about the electric chair, and about all the people reputedly "fried" in it. I am afraid of the school, where all the students seem to be budding criminals.

"What's the matter with your eye?" they ask, critically.

When I don't answer (I cannot decide whether it was an "accident" or not), they shove me, insist on a fight.

My brother, the one who created the story about the wire, comes to my rescue. But then brags so much about "protecting" me, I become sick.

After weeks of torture at the school, my parents decide to send me back to our old community to my old school. I live with my grandparents and the teacher they board. But there is no room for Phoebe, my cat. By the time my grandparents decide there *is* room, and I ask for my cat, she cannot be found. Miss Yarborough, the boarding teacher, takes me under her wing, and begins to teach me to play the piano. But soon she marries an African—a "prince," she says—and is whisked away to his continent.

At my old school there is at least one teacher who loves me. She is the teacher who "knew me before I was born" and bought my first baby clothes. It is she who makes life bearable. It is her presence that finally helps me turn on the one child at the school who continually calls me "one-eyed bitch." One day I simply grab him by his coat and beat him until I am satisfied. It is my teacher who tells me my mother is ill.

My mother is lying in bed in the middle of the day, something I have never seen. She is in too much pain to speak. She has an abscess in her ear. I stand looking down on her, knowing that if she dies, I cannot live. She is being treated with warm oils and hot bricks held against her cheek. Finally a doctor comes. But I must go back to my grandparents' house. The weeks pass, but I am hardly aware of it. All I know is that my mother might die, my father is not so jolly, my brothers still have their guns, and I am the one sent away from home.

"You did not change," they say.

Did I imagine the anguish of never looking up?

I am twelve. When relatives come to visit I hide in my room. My cousin Brenda, just my age, whose father works in the post office and whose mother is a nurse, comes to find me. "Hello," she says. And then she asks, looking at my recent school picture which I did not want taken, and on which the "glob" as I think of it is clearly visible, "You still can't see out of that eye?"

"No," I say, and flop back on the bed over my book.

That night, as I do almost every night, I abuse my eye. I rant and rave at it, in front of the mirror. I plead with it to clear up before morning. I tell it I hate and despise it. I do not pray for sight. I pray for beauty.

"You did not change," they say.

I am fourteen and baby-sitting for my brother Bill who lives in Boston. He is my favorite brother and there is a strong bond between us. Understanding my feelings of shame and ugliness, he and his wife take me to a local hospital where the "glob" is removed by a doctor named O. Henry. There is still a small bluish crater where the scar tissue was, but the ugly white stuff is gone. Almost immediately I become a different person from the girl who does not raise her head. Or so I think. Now that I've raised my head, I win the boyfriend of my dreams. Now that I've raised my head, I have plenty of friends. Now that I've raised my head, classwork comes from my lips as faultlessly as Easter speeches did, and I leave high school as valedictorian, most popular student and *queen,* hardly believing my luck. Ironically, the girl who was voted most beautiful in our class (and was) was later shot twice through the chest by a male companion, using a "real" gun, while she was pregnant. But that's another story in itself. Or, is it?

"You did not change," they say.

It is now thirty years since the "accident." A gorgeous woman and famous journalist comes to visit and to interview me. She is going to write a cover story for her magazine that focuses on my last book. "Decide how you want to look on the cover," she says. "Glamorous, or whatever."

Never mind "glamorous," it is the "whatever" that I hear. Suddenly all I can think of is whether I will get enough sleep the night before the photography session: if I don't, my eye will be tired and wander, as blind eyes will.

At night in bed with my lover I think up reasons why I should not appear on the cover of a magazine. "My meanest critics will say I've sold out," I say. "My family will now realize I write scandalous books." "But what's the real reason you don't want to do this?" he asks.

"Because in all probability," I say in a rush, "my eye won't be straight."

"It will be straight enough," he says. Then, "Besides, I thought you'd made your peace with that."

And I suddenly realize that I have.

I remember:

I am talking to my brother Jimmy, asking if he remembers anything unusual about the day I was shot. He does not know I consider that day the last time my father, with his sweet home remedy of cool lily leaves, "chose" me, and that I suffered rage inside because of this. "Well," he says, "all I remember is standing by the side of the highway with Daddy, trying to flag down a car. A white man stopped, but when Daddy said he needed somebody to take his little girl to the doctor, he drove off."

I remember:

I am thirty-three years old. And in the desert for the first time. I fall totally in love with it. I am so overwhelmed by its beauty, I confront for the first time, consciously, the meaning of the doctor's words years ago: "Eyes are sympathetic. If one is blind, the other will likely become blind too." I realize I have dashed about the world madly, looking at this, looking at that, storing up images against the fading of the light. *But I might have missed seeing the desert!* The shock of that possibility—and gratitude for more than twenty-five years of sight—sends me literally to my knees. Poem after poem comes—which is perhaps how poets pray.

On Sight

I am so thankful I have seen
The Desert
And the creatures in The Desert
And the desert itself.

The desert has its own moon
Which I have seen
With my own eye

There is no flag on it

Trees of the desert have arms
All of which are always up
That is because the moon is up
The sun is up
The stars
Clouds
None with flags.

If there *were* flags, I doubt
the trees would point.
Would you?

But mostly, I remember this:

I am twenty-seven, and my baby daughter is almost three. Since her birth I have worried over her discovery that her mother's eyes are different from other people's. Will she be embarrassed? I wonder. What will she say? Every day she watches a television program called "Big Blue Marble." It begins with a picture of the earth as it appears from the moon. It is bluish, a little battered-looking but full of light, with whitish clouds swirling around it. Every time I see it I weep with love, as if it is a picture of

Grandma's house. One day when I am putting Rebecca down for her nap, she suddenly focuses on my eye. Something inside me cringes, gets ready to try to protect myself. All children are cruel about physical differences, I know from experience, and that they don't always mean to be is another matter. I assume Rebecca will be the same.

But no-o-o-o. She studies my face intently as we stand, her inside and me outside her crib. She even holds my face maternally between her dimpled little hands. Then, looking every bit as serious and lawyerlike as her father, she says, as if it may just possibly have slipped my attention: "Mommy, there's a *world* in your eye." (As in, "Don't be alarmed, or do anything crazy.") And then, gently, but with great interest: "Mommy, where did you *get* that world in your eye?"

For the most part, the pain left then. (So what if my brothers grew up to buy even more powerful pellet guns for their sons. And to carry real guns themselves. So what if a young "Morehouse man" once nearly fell off the steps of Trevor Arnett Library because he thought my eyes were blue.) Crying and laughing I ran to the bathroom, while Rebecca mumbled and sang herself off to sleep. Yes indeed, I realized, looking into the mirror. There *was* a world in my eye. And I saw that it was possible to love it: that in fact, for all it had taught me, of shame and anger and inner vision, I *did* love it. Even to see it drifting out of orbit in boredom, or rolling up out of fatigue, not to mention floating back at attention in excitement (bearing witness, a friend has called it), deeply suitable to my personality, and even characteristic of me.

That night I dream I am dancing to Stevie Wonder's song "Always." As I dance, whirling and joyous, happier than I've ever been in my life, another bright-faced dancer joins me. We dance and kiss each other and hold each other through the night. The other dancer has obviously come through all right, as I have done. She is beautiful, whole and free. And she is also me.

What the Fish Feels

It's different, out there.
Water lifts, bounces me
like a kite. Head empties, fills
with water   fishy
slap   slap
water in my armpits
water surrounding each toe
water under the roots
of my teeth. Gone the stares
the niggling pull of gravity
I can do anything
I will swim forever, holding
the water between my strong thighs
Water slides past my belly
Anxious muscles
lap at it like dogs
This is what the fish feels
this rippling arc
this ecstasy
the slippery sun on my back
water
water
I can do anything

Contributors

Jo Brooks was born in Lebanon, Pennsylvania and now lives near New Haven, Connecticut. The mother of three grown children, she has studied at several colleges, including Barnard. She has been active in the women's movement and, since becoming paraplegic five years ago, the disability rights movement. She is a member of the Anderson Street Writing Workshops and has written poetry since she was sixteen. She is an administrator for IBM, and enjoys gardening, and canoeing.

Dale Brown is a national leader in the self-help movement for people with learning disabilities. She founded the Association of Learning Disabled Adults (ALDA) and the National Network of Learning Disabled Adults (NNLDA). She currently works for the President's Committee on Employment of the Handicapped, writes for *Disabled USA,* and has published over thirty-five articles and essays about her work.

Roberta Cepko was born in 1958 and grew up in Maryland. She graduated from George Washington University in 1983 with a B.A. in English Literature. She is presently an account administrator with IBM in Bethesda, Maryland. She is a short story writer and aspiring novelist.

Joyce Davies lives in San Jose, California and has four children, two grandchildren, and one great-grandchild. Married forty-seven years, she has lived in many different parts of the United States, where she has done volunteer work for schools, churches, the Red Cross, and the League of Women Voters. Her first novel, a romance, was published in the Silhouette First Love series early in 1986. She has also published short stories, articles, and poetry in small press magazines and is currently at work on another book. Her disability is the result of polio contracted at age twenty-six.

Cheryl Davis is a graduate student of journalism at the University of California, Berkeley. She previously worked for the American Association for the Advancement of Science and for the Massachusetts state government. In 1977, Harvard University named her a Loeb Fellow in Environmental Studies. She is currently studying the nature of authority and the abuse of power in American life. Other interests include science, popular culture, and the media. Davis, who is forty, has spina bifida. She lives in Palo Alto, California.

Frances Deloatch speaks frequently to schoolchildren, business people, and medical professionals about disability issues, and is active in the Boston Children's Museum and the Massachusetts Very Special Arts Program. She is also on the advisory boards of the Massachusetts state and city offices of handicapped affairs. Her hobbies include people-watching, swimming, playing with her nephews, and listening to Motown music.

Leslie A. Donovan is a feminist poet and medieval scholar. Now twenty-nine, she was born in Missouri and moved to New Mexico at age fourteen. She is a wheelchair user with juvenile rheumatoid arthritis. She received her B.A. in Creative Writing, and her M.A. in English Literature and Medieval Studies from the University of New Mexico. She was part of a Fulbright group-grant program to the University of Iceland and is currently studying early Irish language and literature in Dublin on an ITT International Fellowship.

Susan Downer, blind since birth, was raised in California's Santa Clara Valley. She received a B.A. in Literature and Creative Writing from the University of California at Santa Cruz and an M.F.A. in English from the University of Massachusetts at Amherst. She currently teaches composition and creative writing at San Jose State University, where she also serves as editor of the disabled student services newsletter. A jazz singer and flutist, she resides in Santa Cruz with her husband.

Carolyn S. Foote was a biology professor, wife of an Episcopal bishop of Idaho, a mother, and a poet. Her disability was arthritis; she made herself play the organ every day to keep her fingers moving. She died in a fire in 1980. Her *Selected Poems* (Cold Drill Books, 1984) were published posthumously by her daughter.

Mary E. Wilkins Freeman was born in 1852 in Randolph, Massachusetts to a family of New England settlers. Although sickly as a child, she graduated in 1870 from Brattleboro (Vermont) High School with an excellent record and briefly attended Mount Holyoke Female Seminary. In the 1880s, she began to publish her short stories in periodicals such as *Harper's Bazaar, Lippincott's,* and the *Atlantic Monthly.* She married Charles

Freeman in 1902. Her later years were affected by a growing hearing loss. She died in 1930 at age seventy-eight, having written twenty volumes of fiction, six collections of children's stories, and innumerable uncollected stories, poems, and articles.

Terry Galloway was born in Stuttgart, Germany and reared in Berlin and Texas. After graduating from the University of Texas, she published a book of poems, co-wrote a PBS series, and helped to found a political cabaret, for which she also served as a director and performer. Her one-woman show, *Heart of a Dog,* was produced in New York and won the Villager Award for Outstanding Solo Performance. In 1985 she received a Dobie Paisano Fellowship from the Texas Institute of Letters to complete her second play.

Rebecca Gordon is a San Francisco poet, feminist activist, and bookkeeper. She is an editor of *Lesbian Contradictions: A Journal of Irreverent Feminism,* and author of *Letters from Nicaragua* (Spinsters/Aunt Lute, 1986), reflections on six months she spent as a volunteer with Witness for Peace, protesting U.S. sponsored attacks on Nicaragua.

Carolyn Hardesty is a graduate student in expository writing and American Studies, and a freshman rhetoric instructor at the University of Iowa. She has published articles, book reviews, and a short story. She is separated from her husband, with whom she shares parenting of her youngest daughter. She reports that although rheumatoid arthritis continues to be part of her life, it now rarely demands primary attention.

Florence Howe, author, editor, educator, and publisher, currently serves as Visiting Professor of English at the Graduate School, The City University of New York, and as Director of The Feminist Press, which she co-founded in 1970. Her numerous publications include *No More Masks! An Anthology of Poems by Women* (Doubleday, 1973), coedited with Ellen Bass, and *Myths of Coeducation* (Indiana University Press, 1985).

Deborah Kendrick lives with her husband and two children in Cincinnati, Ohio. A freelance writer of articles, editorials, and reviews, she is editor of *Tactic,* a computer quarterly for visually impaired people. Her poetry has appeared in *Kaleidoscope, Cincinnati Poetry Review,* and *Dialogue,* and is included in the anthology, *Toward Solomon's Mountain* (Temple University Press, 1986). Named *Cincinnati Enquirer* Woman of the Year for 1985, she has been blind since early childhood.

Debra Kent works full time as a freelance writer. She is the author of numerous book reviews and articles on disability. She also writes young adult fiction. She is blind and lives in Chicago with her husband and young daughter.

Adrienne Lee Lauby grew up in a large Catholic family in the Midwest farmlands. She has a B.A. in English and writes poetry and short stories, and is currently at work on a novel. Thirty-six years old, she has worked for ten years in the feminist and lesbian communities. She has been disabled for four years by severe asthma and digestive problems. She now lives in the Sierra Mountain foothills.

Laurel Lee lectures extensively in the United States and abroad. Her three books were published by E.P. Dutton: *Walking through the Fire: A Hospital Journal* (1977); *Signs of Spring* (1980); and *Mourning into Dancing* (1984). Her articles have appeared in numerous periodicals, including *Family Circle* and the *Washington Post*. She lives with her three children in Topanga, California.

Raymond Lifchez is Professor of Architecture at the University of California, Berkeley. A disability rights advocate, he is co-author, with Barbara Winslow, of the award-winning *Design for Independent Living* (University of California Press, 1979).

Linda McCormick, whose fiber mobile "With Wings" appears on the cover of this book, is a textile sculptor and photographer. As a graduate student in fibers and textile art at the University of Wisconsin, River Falls, she worked under fiber artist Walter Nottingham, and has also studied at Penland School of Crafts, and Syracuse University. She has had nearly thirty exhibits and has received over a dozen awards for her work. Her spinal cord was injured in an accident in 1976.

Nancy Mairs was born in California, reared in New England, and now lives in Tucson, Arizona, where she teaches women's studies and writing at the University of Arizona. She is currently a Visiting Lecturer at the University of California at Los Angeles Writing Programs. Her disabilities are multiple sclerosis and chronic clinical depression. Her work includes *In All the Rooms of the Yellow House* (Blue Moon and Confluence Press, 1984), which won the 1984 Western States Book Award in poetry, and *Plaintext* (University of Arizona Presss, 1986).

Mary Grimley Mason was born in New Jersey in 1928 and lived in Montreal for ten years. Her disability is residual polio from an attack in

1932. She was treated at Warm Springs, Georgia, along with Franklin Roosevelt. She was educated at Radcliffe College and Harvard Graduate School and studied one summer with Irish fiction writer Frank O'Connor. For the last three years, she has been a resident and member of the board of trustees of Commington Community of the Arts, where she is working on a collection of short fiction.

Vassar Miller lives in Houston, Texas, her birthplace and lifelong home. She is a graduate of the University of Houston and has conducted tutorial courses in creative writing at St. John's School. Her volumes of poetry include *Wage War on Silence* (Wesleyan,1960) *Onions and Roses,* (Wesleyan, 1968), and *If I Could Sleep Deeply Enough* (Liveright, 1974), and she is editor of the anthology, *Despite This Flesh: The Disabled in Stories and Poems* (Austin: University of Texas Press, 1985).

Murielle Minard is a wife and the mother of five grown children. Because of restrictions imposed by an early attack of polio, she was educated at home by tutors. She returned to college a few years ago and is now earning a B.A. in English literature. She lives on Long Island in New York, where she is active in community groups for disabled people.

Adrienne Rich was born in 1929 in Baltimore, Maryland, and graduated from Radcliffe College in 1951. The mother of three sons, she lived in Cambridge, Massachusetts, New York City, and western Massachusetts before moving to her current residence in California. She has published more than twelve volumes of poetry and has written extensively on feminism and lesbianism.

Muriel Rukeyser was born in 1913 and was educated at Vassar College and Columbia University. A member of the National Institute of Arts and Letters, and president of PEN, she published fourteen volumes of poetry, as well as a play, TV scripts, a novel, children's books, biographies, criticism, and various translations. Partially paralyzed by a stroke in 1968, she continued to write during and after her recovery. She suffered a second, more serious, stroke in 1977 and died in 1980.

Barbara Ruth lives in the San Francisco Bay area. She is forty years old and describes herself as a psychic, a survivor, a warrior, and a peacemaker, as well as Jewish, Native American, lesbian, and fat, all of which inform her writing. She is seeking a publisher for her two novels and is a member of Wry Crips, a disabled women's readers' theater, and the Jewish Lesbian Writer's Group.

Marsha Saxton currently works as a consultant for The Feminist Press and The Boston Self-Help Center, developing resources for disabled women. A trainer and organizer in peer counseling for people with disabilities, she has also lectured widely about disability issues and reproductive technologies. A native of California, she now resides in a cooperative house in Boston, where she helps care for her godchild and where she makes patchwork quilts. Her disability is spina bifida.

Jean Stewart, writer, disability rights organizer, and wheelchair-user, lives in upstate New York. She is executive director of an independent living center she founded three years ago and president of the Access Institute. In addition to her work on behalf of disabled people, she has been active in the women's movement, the anti-war movement, and in farmworker and tenant organizing. In 1981, she edited *Sing Out!* magazine's special issue on the folk music and culture of people with disabilities. Her writings have appeared in *Hanging Loose, Women's Studies Quarterly,* and *Disability Rag.* The poems and prose included in *With Wings* are all excerpted from her work, *The Body's Memory.*

Carol Stone is Associate Professor of English at Montclair State College, where she teaches courses in women's literature and creative writing. She is currently working on her fourth chapbook of poems, and writing essays on contemporary women poets. Her essay on Kate Chopin's *The Awakening* appeared in *Women's Studies.*

Alice Walker was born in Eatonton, Georgia, the eighth child of a family of sharecroppers. Educated at Spelman College and Sarah Lawrence College, she is a teacher, black studies scholar, poet, and novelist. Among her several volumes of prose and poetry is the Pulitzer-Prize-winning *The Color Purple* (Harcourt Brace Jovanovich, 1982). She is also founder and publisher of Wild Trees Press.

Kay Yasutome has a B.A. in English from Portland State University, and has studied with poet Sandra McPherson. She received a grant with two other Oregon writers from the Oregon Arts Commissions to establish the first Oregon Disabled Writer Project, which produced a combined portfolio of their work. Her disability is multiple sclerosis. She is a two-time recipient winner of *Kaleidoscope's* International Poetry, Fiction and Art Awards.

Miriam Ylvisaker lives in the San Francisco Bay area where she has taught for fifteen years at Oakland High School. A writer and editor, her articles and stories have appeared in *American Home, Infoworld, English Journal, Phi Delta Kappan, Kansas Quarterly,* and *Descant.*

Acknowledgments

Dale Brown. "Learning to Work" first appeared in *American Rehabilitation* 9: 1 (1983).

Roberta Cepko. "On Oxfords and Plaster Casts" is reprinted by permission of the author from the *Washington Post,* May 13, 1984. © 1984 by Roberta Cepko.

Leslie A. Donovan. "For a Paralyzed Woman Raped and Murdered while Alone in Her Own Apartment" first appeared in *Women's Studies Quarterly* 13: 3 & 4 (Fall/Winter 1985).

Carolyn S. Foote. "Arthritis" is reprinted by permission of the publisher from *Selected Poems* by Carolyn S. Foote (Boise, ID: Cold Drill Books, 1984). © 1984 by Cold Drill Books.

Terry Galloway, "I'm Listening as Hard as I Can" is reprinted with permission from the April 1981 issue of *Texas Monthly.* © 1981 by *Texas Monthly.*

Rebecca Gordon. "By Her Hands" is reprinted by permission of the author from *Sinister Wisdom,* No. 19 (Winter 1982), P.O. Box 1308, Montpelier, VT 05602. © 1982 by Rebecca Gordon.

Deborah Kendrick. "20/20 with a Twist" is reprinted by permission of the author from *The Braille Forum* 22: 2 (August 1983). © 1983 by Deborah Kendrick. "For Tess Gallagher" is reprinted by permission of the author from *Kaleidoscope,* Fall 1982. © 1982 by Deborah Kendrick.

Debra Kent. "In Search of Liberation" first appeared in *Disabled USA* 1: 3 (1977).

Laurel Lee, Excerpt from *Walking through the Fire: A Hospital Journal* (New York: Dutton, 1977) is reprinted by permission of the publisher, E.P. Dutton, a division of New American Library. © 1977 by Laurel Lee.

Raymond Lifchez and Cheryl Davis. Excerpt from "Living Upstairs, Leaving Home, and at the Moscow Circus," is reprinted by permission of the publisher from "What Every Architect Should Know" in *Disabled People as Second-Class Citizens,* ed. by M.G. Eisenberg, C. Griggins, and R. J. Duval (New York: Springer, 1982). © 1982 by Springer Publishing Co, Inc.

Nancy Mairs. "Diminishment" first appeared in a pamphlet published by Walter F. Stromer, Mount Vernon, IA 52314. © 1978 by Nancy

Mairs. Reprinted by permission of the author. "Conversations at All Hours" is reprinted by permission of the author from *In All the Rooms of the Yellow House* (Lewiston, ID: Blue Moon and Confluence Press, Lewis and Clark State College, 1984). © 1984 by Nancy Mairs. "Shape" first appeared in *Intro 13* (Associated Writing Programs), Old Dominion University, Norfolk, VA and in *Kaleidoscope,* Spring 1985. © 1985 by Nancy Mairs. Reprinted by permission of the author. "On Being a Cripple" first appeared in *MSS,* published by the State University of New York at Binghamton, Binghamton, NY, and is included in *Plaintext* by Nancy Mairs (Tucson, AZ: University of Arizona Press, 1986). © 1986 by the Arizona Board of Regents. Reprinted by permission of the author and publisher.

Vassar Miller. "Insomniac's Prayer," "Faux Pas," and "Love Story for Easter Even" are reprinted by permission of the author from *If I Could Sleep Deeply Enough* by Vassar Miller (New York: Liveright, 1974).

Adrienne Rich. "Transit" is reprinted from *The Fact of a Doorframe: Poems Selected and New, 1950-1984* by Adrienne Rich. By permission of the author and W.W. Norton & Co. Inc. © 1984 by Adrienne Rich. © 1975, 1978 by W.W. Norton & Co. Inc. © 1981 by Adrienne Rich. "A Woman Dead in Her Forties" is reprinted from *The Dream of a Common Language, Poems 1974-1977* by Adrienne Rich. By permission of the author and the publisher. © 1978 by W.W. Norton & Co. Inc.

Muriel Rukeyser. "Resurrection of the Right Side," "St. Roach," "Mendings," and "The Wards" are reprinted by permission of International Creative Management from *The Gates* by Muriel Rukeyser (New York: McGraw Hill, 1976).

Marsha Saxton. Excerpt from "The Something That Happened before I Was Born" is reprinted by permission of the author from *Ordinary Moments,* ed. by Alan Brightman (Syracuse, NY: Human Policy Press, 1982). © 1982 by Marsha Saxton.

Alice Walker. "Beauty: When the Other Dancer Is the Self" is reprinted by permission of the author and publisher from *In Search of Our Mothers' Gardens* by Alice Walker (New York: Harcourt Brace Jovanovich, 1983). © 1983 by Alice Walker.

Kay Yasutome. "I Met Florence in Room 43" is reprinted by permission of the author from *The Oregon Disabled Writers' Project* (Portland, OR: Trask House Books, 1984). © 1984 by Kay Yasutome.